HOGAN
THE MAN
WHO PLAYED
FOR GLORY

HOGAN

THE MAN WHO PLAYED FOR GLORY

by Gene Gregston

Prentice-Hall, Inc., Englewood Cliffs, New Jersey

For PATRICIA,
who had confidence, faith, hope
and an abundance of charity.

Hogan: The Man Who Played for Glory, by Gene Gregston
Copyright © 1978 by Gene Gregston

Printed in the United States of America
Prentice-Hall International, Inc., London
Prentice-Hall of Australia, Pty. Ltd., Sydney
Prentice-Hall of Canada, Ltd., Toronto
Prentice-Hall of India Private Ltd., New Delhi
Prentice-Hall of Japan, Inc., Tokyo
Prentice-Hall of Southeast Asia Pte. Ltd., Singapore
Whitehall Books Limited, Wellington, New Zealand
10 9 8 7 6 5 4 3 2

Library of Congress Cataloging in Publication Data

Gregston, Gene,
  Hogan: the man who played for glory.

  Includes index.
  1. Hogan, Ben, 1912-   2. Golfers—United
States—Biography.
GV964.H6G73   796.352'092'4 [B]   77-27421
ISBN 0-13-392464-5

Acknowledgments

Many people contributed to the writing of this book, and all have my sincere gratitude, especially these:

In Colorado—Dick Connor.

In Florida—Bud Harvey, Dick Hale, Gardner Dickinson, Tommy Bolt.

In Georgia—Wilda Gwin.

In New Mexico—Pat and Max Evans.

In New York—Herbert Warren Wind, Joseph C. Dey, Fred Corcoran, Dan Jenkins.

In North Carolina—Irwin Smallwood.

In Texas—Jim Trinkle, Al Panzera, Flem Hall, Buster Brannon, Charlcia
Bullard, Bobby Malone, Raymond Gafford, Frances Walker,
Gene Strahan, Bill Bellamy, Bob Ostrum, Penny and Buddy
Branum, June and Frank Underwood.
And in California—
Paul Sutherland for his persistence;
My daughter Donna, her husband, Dan Rahilly, and my son
Patrick for consistently positive attitudes;
Diane and John Sinor, Connie and Ralph Yoes, for encourage-
ment, friendship, and fire ring companionship;
Dr. Albert L. Anderson, Norman Roberts, and Carl Lichty for
being three old friends who were tried and stayed true;
Anne and Jean DeMeules for all of the above and more.

Gene Gregston
Viejas Indian Reservation

The following publishers and individuals graciously granted permission
to reprint selected material:

The Story of American Golf, by Herbert Warren Wind, published
by Simon & Schuster, Inc. Copyright © 1956 by Herbert Warren Wind.
Reprinted by permission of Herbert Warren Wind.

The Realm of Sport, edited by Herbert Warren Wind, published
by Simon & Schuster, Inc. Reprinted by permission of Herbert Warren
Wind.

The Story of the Augusta National Golf Club, by Clifford
Roberts, published by Doubleday & Company, Inc. Copyright © 1976
by Clifford Roberts. Reprinted by permission of Clifford Roberts.

The Education of a Golfer, by Sam Snead with Al Stump, published by Simon & Schuster, Inc. Copyright © 1962 by Sam Snead and
Al Stump. Reprinted by permission of Simon & Schuster, Inc.

Thirty Years of Championship Golf, by Gene Sarazen with Herbert Warren Wind, published by Prentice-Hall, Inc. Copyright 1950 by
Prentice-Hall, Inc. Reprinted by permission of the publisher.

Power Golf, by Ben Hogan, published by A. S. Barnes & Co.,
Inc. Copyright 1948 by A. S. Barnes & Co., Inc. Reprinted by permission of the publisher.

The Modern Fundamentals of Golf, by Ben Hogan, published by
A. S. Barnes & Co., Inc. Copyright © 1957 by Ben Hogan. Reprinted by
permission of A. S. Barnes & Co., Inc.

1

I have always thought of golf as the best of all games—the most interesting, the most demanding, the most rewarding. I cannot begin to express the satisfaction I have always felt in being part of a game with such a wonderful flavor and spirit, a game which has produced such superb champions and attractive personalities as Harry Vardon, Francis Ouimet, Bob Jones, Walter Hagen, Gene Sarazen, Tommy Armour, Sam Snead, Byron Nelson, Jimmy Demaret—to name only a few of the great players. I have found the game to be, in all factualness, a universal language wherever I traveled at home or abroad.

I have really enjoyed every minute I have spent in golf—above all, the many wonderful friends I have made. I have loved playing the game and practicing it. Whether my schedule for the following day called for a tournament round or merely a trip to the practice tee, the prospect that there was going to be golf in it made me feel privileged and extremely happy, and I couldn't wait for the sun to come up the next morning so that I could get out on the course again./Ben Hogan, 1957

Neither a tournament nor a practice session was on Ben Hogan's schedule when the wake-up call came at 6:30 that morning, yet he still had every reason to feel privileged and happy. At thirty-six he was the best golfer in the world, and his future was rich with promise.

Within two hours, however, that future was almost obliterated when a bus hurtled head on into his car on a foggy West Texas highway. Four weeks later Hogan's condition was so critical that a news wire service distributed an obituary story about him to newspapers and radio stations, for use in case of his death. His success in golf, slow in coming, now seemed cruelly and quickly ended.

Ben Hogan had made it to the top the hard way, enduring years of failure and struggle. But by 1948 when he won the United States Open, the Professional Golfers' Association championship, and the Western Open—the only golfer to have collected those three titles in the same year—he had reached the pinnacle.

In the first month of the new year, furthermore, Hogan had shown every intention of remaining there by winning two of the first four tournaments. Indeed, Hogan had won eleven of the last sixteen tournaments he had entered. Ben believed he now had the "touch" he had long been seeking, that elusive "feel" for the game which instilled the confidence that he could score well every time he teed up the ball.

Ben and his wife Valerie were anticipating completion of the drive from Phoenix to Fort Worth and settling into their new home, their first in fourteen years of marriage. Hogan planned a few weeks' vacation from the tournament circuit.

"It isn't the golf, it's the traveling," he had said three weeks earlier in explaining his decision to cut back on his playing schedule. Then he added, "I want to die an old man, not a young man."

Ben left Room 217 and went downstairs to the lobby of the El Capitan Hotel, largest building in the small West Texas town of Van Horn. It was about five minutes to seven, and the calendar hanging on the wall near desk clerk Dorothy Evans read: "Wednesday, Feb. 2, 1949." Hogan walked out to his nearly new Cadillac and drove it across Highway 80 to a service station.

Eighty miles to the east in Pecos, Texas, Alvin H. Logan, twenty-seven years old, leaped up the steps of bus number 548, greeted the thirty-four passengers with a hearty "Good morning!" took the driver's seat, and began shifting the idling engine into gear.

A lady sitting near the front asked, "Young man, when will we get to El Paso?"

"About noon," Logan replied. "It's about two hundred ten miles. Usually make it in five hours if we stay on schedule." At seven o'clock, right on schedule, the Dallas–El Paso bus rolled out onto Highway 80 heading west.

Logan was a substitute driver for the Greyhound Bus Company. He was based in Pecos and averaged making the Pecos–El Paso leg of the route three times a week.

Hogan drove back to the hotel and parked. He went next door and bought an El Paso newspaper, then entered the hotel coffee shop for breakfast. Valerie remained in the room, skipping breakfast because she was suffering from the travel sickness that plagued her throughout the many journeys with her husband.

As he ate breakfast, Hogan read the sports section. There was a short story noting that Ben Hogan was the official PGA money-winning leader after the first month of the tour with two victories, plus a second in Monday's play-off with Jimmy Demaret in the Phoenix Open.

There was a twinge of regret at not having won the

Phoenix play-off with Demaret—Hogan wanted to win every tournament he entered. But he recognized the futility of that desire.

Overall, January had been a fine month. Including the matching bonuses from MacGregor Sporting Goods when he won a tournament as a member of the advisory staff, Ben had grossed more than $11,000 through four events.

He left the coffee shop, went to the room, picked up the suitcases, and with Valerie checked out of the El Capitan at 7:42 A.M. Hogan paid the night's rent of $4.50, loaded the luggage and his clubs into the back seat of the Cadillac, and drove out of Van Horn shortly after eight o'clock.

Highway 80 east of Van Horn was a straight two-lane stretch for several miles. Ground fog lay like a white blanket across the landscape, a common occurrence in the cold, clear early mornings of winter in the area of the Pecos River Valley.

The fog limited visibility, but traffic was light, the road flat, and Hogan soon had the Cadillac speeding toward Fort Worth.

Alvin Logan braked the bus to a stop at a service station in Kent, a small town thirty-seven miles east of Van Horn. He picked up a bundle of Fort Worth *Star-Telegram*s and started to throw it from the driver's window. But he feared the bundle would break so he decided to carry the papers out of the bus and place them between two of the pumps.

Because of this delay, Logan found an Alamo Freight Line semitrailer truck in front of him when he drove the bus back onto the highway.

The Alamo freighter was driven by Hubert H. Harshaw of San Antonio, and he was in no hurry since Highway 80 west of Kent twisted and turned and dipped through the southern foothills of the Apache Mountains and was not a section of highway designed for high speed. Numerous blind hills and curves made passing a risk in the best of weather, and this morning the fog compounded that risk. Both Harshaw and Logan had turned on their headlights, but the beams did not aid the drivers' visibility.

4

The Hogans had been on the road about fifteen minutes when another factor was added to the expanding equation. Ben turned to Valerie and said, "I think we have a flat tire." Ben slowed the car and stopped on the shoulder of the highway. He got out and walked around the Cadillac checking the tires. They were all right, but he noticed small patches of ice on the pavement and realized they had caused his difficulty in controlling the automobile.

Hogan switched on the headlights and drove at a speed reduced to what he later described as "practically nothing."

Logan, the bus driver, was becoming impatient. He had been trailing the Alamo freighter for six or seven miles and was falling behind schedule. Logan knew, and later said, that even in clear weather "there really isn't any place you make a pass and make it safely."

He planned to try it anyway. As the truck, then the bus, topped a rise, Logan thought he could see two to three hundred yards ahead. The road ran down into a shallow valley, across a culvert built over a dry wash, and up the opposite hill. The bridge-culvert had guard rails of cement running alongside the highway to prevent vehicles from plunging off into the wash.

But the valley, wash, and culvert were obscured by the fog. So was the black Cadillac coming down the other side of the valley.

Logan shifted the bus into third gear to get more snap as he veered left to move by the truck. According to the governor on the bus, the speed in third gear ranged from thirty-three to thirty-eight miles per hour. Logan pulled abreast of the truck and shifted into fourth gear. The bus was on the downgrade and picking up speed.

Ben Hogan suddenly saw four lights facing him from out of the fog. He realized the situation instantly and wheeled the Cadillac to the right. But there was the concrete abutment running across the wash. He could not get off the highway. Ben yelled, "Look out, Valerie!" and flung his body to the right across his wife.

Logan jerked the bus back toward the westbound lane, but not soon enough. The left front of the bus smashed into the left front of the Cadillac. The bus weighed 19,250 pounds; the Cadillac weighed 3,900 pounds.

The jarring collision jolted the Cadillac backward, and it bounced and skidded sideways to the right. The steering wheel was rocketed through the front seat into the back seat, thrusting through the space occupied only seconds before by Hogan. It caught his left shoulder, breaking the collarbone. The engine of the Cadillac was slammed back into the driver's area, mangling Ben's left leg and smashing into his stomach.

Hogan's evasive dive out of the path of the steering wheel not only achieved his purpose of protecting Valerie but undoubtedly saved his own life.

Harshaw knew the bus had struck something but did not know what. He jackknifed his truck into the embankment to the north of the highway to avoid ramming the rear of the Greyhound.

Ricocheting off the Cadillac, the bus careened out of control across the highway, banged and rattled along a drainage ditch and finally lurched to a stop against an embankment, about 333 feet beyond the point of the crash.

Logan's broken watch had stopped at 8:30 A.M.

The bus passengers, none hurt seriously, staggered out and stood around numbly in the eerie fog.

Hogan, barely conscious, lay across Valerie's lap. The luggage had tumbled from the back seat into the front seat. Valerie, with cuts and bruises about the head and numerous lacerations on her legs, was trapped by the position of her husband and luggage and could not move.

Almost an hour passed before the two of them were helped out of the car. Hogan lay by the side of the road, a blanket providing some warmth for his battered body.

Highway patrolmen George Summerhill and A. A. Montgomery of the Texas Department of Public Safety arrived and took command. Summerhill radioed for an ambulance, and Montgomery began the routine investigation for an accident report.

Hogan's golf clubs had been scattered about by the wreck and the efforts to remove the couple from the car. Valerie asked Summerhill if he would gather the clubs for her.

"Yes, ma'am," Summerhill replied, and he started picking up golf clubs. He glanced at Hogan lying by the road, then at Valerie. Valerie did not miss his meaning—the patrolman doubted that Hogan would ever again have use for the golf clubs.

"Why couldn't you have been a little more careful?" Valerie asked the bus driver. "Just look what you have caused."

"Your car was on the wrong side of the road, lady," Logan protested. "You were skidding into me."

Valerie walked away, and kneeled beside her husband.

An ambulance arrived with Dr. John P. Wright, an osteopathic physician from Van Horn who administered first aid to Ben, then Valerie.

At Van Horn Dr. Wright telephoned El Paso and alerted Dr. Lester C. Fenner that he was bringing Ben Hogan to the Hotel Dieu Hospital (loosely translated from the French as Inn of God).

Dr. Wright had referred patients to Fenner in the past, and the hospital staff was prepared when the ambulance arrived at 1:45 P.M.

Word of the accident swept across the country, word that was not always accurate in those first hours. There were reports Hogan had been killed or was not expected to live.

Ben contributed to the uncertainty and speculation about his condition when he asked Dr. Fenner not to issue any statement regarding his injuries until his older brother, Royal, arrived by plane from Fort Worth that evening.

George Hoskins, a former newsman, was the part-time public relations director for the hospital and was trying to be helpful as the media representatives scrambled through the hospital seeking information and photographs.

Sister Josephine, working in the administrative office, complained.

"George," she told Hoskins, "we've got to shoo these people out of here. They're disrupting the entire hospital."

"No," said Hoskins, "that's their job."

The news people stayed. Despite the tightness of the time

7

element, the afternoon's El Paso *Herald-Post* had a fairly accurate, but not complete, story, which ran under the lead page one headline: "Ben Hogan, Golf Star, Injured in Auto Crash."

Hogan told one reporter who managed to see him, "I am lucky to be alive." Valerie and Dr. Fenner agreed. Another reporter conducted an even shorter interview.

"How do you feel?" the reporter asked.

"Not bad," Hogan replied.

As knowledge of Hogan's injuries broadened through examination and X rays, Dr. Fenner called in other physicians. These included Dr. David Cameron, Dr. Leopoldo Villareal, and Dr. J. Leighton Green. Dr. Howard Ditto, Hogan's doctor in Fort Worth, also flew to El Paso to join the team.

That evening, after Royal Hogan arrived and was consulted, Dr. Fenner issued the first report on Hogan's condition, stating that he was known at the time to have suffered a fractured pelvis, broken collarbone, and a deep gash near his left eye.

"We are very much pleased at his progress," the report continued. "We feel sure that he has no other fractures, though a minute X-ray study may reveal a broken rib. We feel sure no surgery will be required."

Further X-ray study revealed not only a broken rib but a broken ankle and a bladder injury. And there were massive contusions in Hogan's left leg.

The next day, Thursday, Valerie quoted Ben as saying, "I'm glad I'll be able to play golf again."

Hogan sent a message to newsmen that he was deeply touched by the many flowers, letters, and telegrams that were filling up Room 301 of the hospital. His golf clubs were propped in a corner so he could see them from the bed. Valerie asked the nurses to distribute some of the flowers to other patients.

Ben Hogan was a tough man. Although weighing only 138 pounds at the time of the accident, Hogan had a wiry, solid, and well-muscled body. His recovery was progressing rapidly even as he lay in a cast up to his waist, and doctors decided Hogan could leave the hospital on February 16. Reporters pressed for an interview before his departure, but Hogan answered, "I have nothing to say."

Mrs. Hattie Collins was spending the winter in El Paso. She lived in Dalhart, in the Texas Panhandle, but in the 1920s had been a resident of Fort Worth and a regular golfer at Glen Garden Country Club.

Among her caddies in those years were "two boys, one tall and lanky, the other a little boy with a wistful look on his face. They happened to be Byron Nelson and Bennie Hogan."

As a friendly gesture, Mrs. Collins went to a newsstand in El Paso on Sundays and bought a *Star-Telegram* to take to Ben in the hospital. Otherwise, he would not receive delivery of the Sunday paper until Tuesday. Mrs. Collins saw Ben the Sunday before he was scheduled to leave the hospital.

"He was sitting up in bed looking wonderful and talking to his doctor and his wife," Mrs. Collins reported.

The next Sunday, however, Ben was still in the hospital, and Mrs. Collins came away from a brief visit with tears in her eyes. She did not exepct ever to see Ben alive again.

Ben had become seriously ill, and the scheduled dismissal had been canceled. After two days of intensive X-ray scanning, the reason was discovered that Sunday night. A small blood clot had reached Hogan's right lung.

Doctors Fenner, Green, and Villareal met. Dr. Green, the internist, presented his findings and diagnosis.

"He has had a pulmonary embolism," Dr. Green informed his colleagues. "Fortunately, the clot was small enough to pass through the pulmonary artery into the lung. The next one could be fatal. A larger clot might form in his left leg and move up and obstruct the artery completely. It is damn bad. He is seriously ill, no question about it. I think it will be touch and go to save him."

"Put full-time monitoring on him," Dr. Fenner said. "I want continual X rays of his left leg. If another clot forms, we must know immediately. Who's the best man in the country at venae cavae?"

A clot moving from the leg had to travel through the vena cava, the large vein of the stomach, to reach the heart. A "vena cava," as Dr. Fenner called it, is an operation that involves ligation of the stomach vein. It was not a common surgical practice in 1949, and no one knew the long-range aftereffects.

"Why don't you call Mayo and ask them?" Dr. Green suggested. "Maybe Barker knows. I think the man in New Orleans is the best but I'm not that familiar with it. There aren't too many venae cavae being done."

Dr. Alton Oschner of New Orleans was recommended.

Valerie moved into the hospital to begin a vigil that would last three weeks.

On Wednesday, February 23, highway patrolman George Summerhill filed Complaint No. 417 at the Culberson County Courthouse in Van Horn. The state of Texas accused Alvin Logan of aggravated assault "causing injury less than death to the person of the said William Ben Hogan."

But even as the complaint was filed, serious doubts existed as to the ultimate result of the injuries. The massive contusions in Hogan's left leg were a grave threat to his life.

At midnight on Wednesday, March 2, a second blood clot was discovered in Hogan's leg. His condition was critical, and the news spread.

The Associated Press transmitted a sixteen-paragraph obituary on Hogan to member newspapers and radio stations.

A message preceded the story: "Editor: The following is a biographical sketch of Ben Hogan, professional golfer, now ill at El Paso. It is intended primarily for use in event of his death, but excerpts may be used as background for current stories. Please preserve this copy. It will not be repeated."

Hogan's doctors agreed that a vena cava operation was necessary to prevent the second clot from moving up to Hogan's heart. With Valerie's approval, Dr. Fenner contacted Dr. Oschner. Oschner was a professor of surgery at Tulane University and chief of staff of the famed Oschner Clinic in New Orleans.

Immediate surgery was recommended. But a rainstorm had grounded all commercial airline flights in New Orleans. Valerie telephoned Forbes Air Base at Topeka, Kansas, and asked for General David W. Hutchinson, the commanding officer. Hutchinson had recently transferred to Forbes from El Paso's Biggs Field, where he had been the CO at the time of the Hogans' accident. Valerie explained the situation to Hutchinson, making a point of her husband's Air Corps service in World War II.

A B-29 bomber on a training flight from Forbes was ordered to New Orleans to pick up Oschner and fly him to El Paso. Dr. Oschner arrived at the Hotel Dieu Hospital about eight o'clock Thursday evening.

Hogan was weak, and there was some concern about his being strong enough to undergo surgery. Valerie wanted him to make the decision. Dr. Oschner carefully explained the operation to Ben, telling him what would be done and how, and what it would mean.

Hogan raised his head slightly to ask one question: "Will I be able to use my legs and play golf?"

Dr. Oschner replied that he was certain of it.

And Ben said, "All right."

Hogan was wheeled into the operating room. Valerie went to the hospital chapel.

Assisted by Doctors Green and Villareal, Oschner operated on Hogan for two hours, tying off the vena cava so that no blood clots could be carried to Hogan's heart or lungs. At midnight Oschner was on a chartered plane returning to New Orleans.

Hogan awoke to find a heavy cast encasing him from hips to armpits. His left leg was swollen and scarred. Blood circulation in his legs was impaired, and he would be given six blood transfusions in the coming days. But the operation had saved his life.

Many of those familiar with the usual rigors of tournament golf and the further demands Hogan made on himself did not think Hogan could ever come back. His being able to walk even nine holes of a golf course after such an ordeal seemed absurd.

Charles Bartlett of the Chicago *Tribune* and Herb Graffis, editor of *Golfing* and *Golfdom* magazines, were two of the senior golf writers in the United States. Both visited Hogan within a few days of the surgery.

"I left the hospital sick at heart, stomach, and head," said Graffis, "but hoping for a miracle."

"Here was a gaunt wisp of a man, seated in an ambulatory walker," said Bartlett, "his ankles swollen because of the circulatory condition. . . . I learned then that Hogan aimed to play again, or at least he was going to give it the old Hogan try. Frankly, I wondered if Ben would walk again."

But most of the people whose messages to Hogan filled five boxes were not so pessimistic. They believed Hogan would return to competitive golf, and one person wrote, "You can do it on one leg, Ben."

Valerie soon learned that her husband agreed with the fans, and he asked for a couple of rubber balls so he could start exercising his hands. The cast was removed a week later, and on March 14 Ben Hogan rolled his wheelchair out onto the grounds of the hospital and enjoyed sunshine for the first time in a month and a half.

He would say in the next few weeks that golf was the farthest thing from his mind and that he was only interested in getting well. But golf was never far from Hogan's mind. Down deep he was committed to the philosophy he expressed in 1946.

"I don't ever expect to quit tournament golf as long as I live," he had said then. "I'm a pro golfer. That's my business. I guess I'll play golf as long as I can drag a leg out there."

Three years later, even that kind of golf was considered a remote possibility for Ben Hogan.

2

Ben has shown me more willpower through this terrible spell than he ever did on a golf course./Valerie Hogan, 1949

As his body began the ever-so-slow mending process, Ben Hogan undertook some soul-searching.

　　　Through the years various golf writers and sports columnists had castigated him in print because of his Sphinx-like reception to their queries or conversational initiatives. They described him as uncooperative, aloof, cold. And those were the more flattering adjectives. Grantland Rice, often referred to as the dean of sports writers during his career, once characterized Ben as being "soft as a fire hydrant."

The writers were reflecting the opinion of many golf fans. Hogan had not let the barbs concern him very much. If he did, he kept that concealed like most of his other emotions.

He was not an introvert. If he felt obliged to express a strong opinion, he did so. But he had found it necessary for success in golf to retreat into introversion, the direction or concentration of one's interest upon oneself.

Hogan had learned that any deviation from this one-dimensional fixity on the game cost him strokes. And he was on the course to make golf shots, not friends.

He related to galleries as if he were playing in a vacuum. His vision was confined to the white ball, the verdant expanse from tee to green, and whatever traps, bunkers, or rough there were to negotiate along the way.

While walking from a green to the next tee on a tournament round, Hogan could pass within two feet of a close acquaintance, stare the person in the eyes without so much as a hint of recognition, and later not recall having seen that person at all.

A fan jingling coins in a pocket or the whirr of a movie camera could startle Hogan out of his trance, however. Of course, his reaction on those occasions merely polarized any trend to antipathy between the crowd and him.

The American sports public, perhaps particularly so in the years after World War II, wanted its heroes to be both superhuman and human—skillful and personable, happy in victory, philosophical in rare defeat. There had been enough grimness in the recent past.

And here was Hogan, a hero whose very trademark was a grim countenance. Tight-lipped, occasionally brusque, rarely smiling, reserved in all relationships—hardly the components of which the public wished its heroes molded.

Hogan basically was shy and modest. He was neither a quipster nor a joke teller. The word "charisma" was not in most dictionaries of the period and Hogan offered the lexicographers no incentive to include it.

Those watching Hogan play golf had to be content with

repeated samples of superior shot making. That was the show. There were no frills.

Hogan had begun to realize he had not been a popular champion. He had thought for some time that the majority of people did not like him. Whether he exaggerated this in his mind, Ben's judgment as usual was sound. He had given only a few people the opportunity to know him, fewer still the opportunity to like him.

Hogan said this had disturbed him in the past. But Valerie believed her husband first began thinking seriously about the subject during the time of introspection in the hospital.

Where the critics of the media had failed, the thousands of goodwill messages succeeded. Hogan, deeply moved by the expressions of kindness, began to feel that most people who admired his golfing ability also were prepared to like him as a person if given any chance to do so. He decided he must learn to acknowledge those multitudes.

"If I ever get out of here," he said to Valerie one day, "I'm going to be more aware of people—and their kindness to me."

It would be a marked departure from the past for Hogan. He would never get closer than a full brassie shot off a tufted lie to being an extrovert. But eventually he would become somewhat more approachable, somewhat less unbending, somewhat friendlier, and, as he promised Valerie, somewhat more aware of people.

The change was so subtle that many people possibly were never cognizant of it. His intensity on the golf course did not diminish, and that is where a majority of people saw Hogan—when he was at work. He would be acclaimed throughout the United States and most of the world and become a sports idol for millions. But Hogan would never lose his reputation as a cold, hard man.

He was a good patient and followed his physicians' prescribed regimen precisely. They liked him and admired his self-discipline and determination. The nurses liked him, too. Happy to be alive, Ben was cooperative and cheerful.

Only the hospital chef had any complaint. Hogan discovered that a downtown restaurant made flapjacks exactly as he liked them, so they were imported to the hospital every morning for his breakfast. Hogan's appetite and his near-fanatical finickiness with the preparation of his food were already legendary among the touring golf professionals.

If he ordered scrambled eggs, the chef was forewarned to cook them in cream, not milk. Kitchen staffs in hotels throughout the country had experienced Hogan's displeasure in the form of a tray or plate returned from the coffee shop, restaurant, or his room along with meticulous instructions on how the meal should be prepared. Nor was Hogan averse to going into the kitchen himself to personally inform the chef how he wanted a dish prepared.

The doctors decided Hogan was well enough to be dismissed from Hotel Dieu Hospital, and arrangements were made for the trip to Fort Worth on the Texas and Pacific Railroad's *Texas Eagle* leaving El Paso at 12:30 A.M., April 1.

Ben and Valerie rode to the station in an automobile. Hogan, wearing white pajamas and a polka-dot bathrobe, was aided by porters and friends on the walk down the car to his compartment. There, holding a handrail, he stood alone for the first time for the benefit of photographers.

The Hogans arrived in Fort Worth. Ben, hollow-cheeked and thin, was lowered from the rear car of the train. He was greeted by applause from a small group gathered to welcome him, and a broad smile creased his features.

Exploding flash bulbs marked the route as he was wheeled and carried along the tracks and down the steps to the cavernous waiting room where he had sold newspapers as a boy. Friends rushed to shake the left hand Hogan offered from beneath the reddish-brown blanket wrapped about him.

Clara Hogan, his mother, tried to hold back tears as she hovered anxiously near him.

An ambulance carried Hogan to the new home at 24 Valley Ridge Road.

Royal and an attendant wheeled Ben to what had been an empty bedroom now converted to a hospital room. More flowers and messages awaited him. Settled in bed, Hogan was in good humor and talked with newsmen.

The doctors told Hogan it would be at least five months before the swelling in his legs disappeared. They advised him that the only way he could build strength in his legs was by walking.

Hogan devised his own routine to accomplish that. He usually awoke about 10, ate breakfast, then went to the living room to walk laps. A "lap" was once around the room, and he hoped to add five laps each morning.

On April 5 he put on an overcoat over his pajamas, wore a billed cap, and took a short stroll in the backyard. Thereafter, if the weather was warm, he went outside and walked around the garden in the afternoons, sometimes watering plants from a pan of water he carried. Then he rested, had dinner, and spent the evenings watching television, reading, writing letters, or visiting with family and friends.

Delta Air Lines Captain Oramel Wright flew to Fort Worth and made a surprise presentation to Hogan on April 7, a photograph of the entire Masters Tournament field and an engraved humidor.

The inscription on the photo read: "To our friend, Ben Hogan. On the eve of the 1949 Masters we sent you heartfelt good wishes for a speedy and complete recovery."

On Easter Sunday, April 17, Hogan dressed in street clothes for the first time since the accident and did fifty-five laps around the living room. He had spent considerable time pondering possibilities for his future, but was not optimistic about returning to championship form.

"I don't see how I can ever get back to the edge that I had last year," he said. "Last year was my best year and I was going good again this year.

"Winning golf is a matter of touch. It's something you work at and try to develop, but you don't develop it. It just comes to you.

"It's the difference between a first-rate golfer and the fellow who scores good once in a while. Once you've got the touch you're set. Even if you make a bad shot now and then, you know you've still got it. The good golfer has got the touch, he knows he can do it."

A well-meaning friend astounded the Hogans by inquiring, "How many rounds has Ben played?"

"I'm just not as well as a lot of people think," Hogan said. "It will be a long time before I even touch a golf club."

On April 30 the Hogans were in New Orleans, where Ben underwent a checkup by Dr. Oschner. The medical reports were encouraging.

"They say I'm going to be all right," Hogan related. "But you have to play tournament golf to know what it is. Sure, I'll probably be all right to go downtown and sit in an office every day. It's like Joe DiMaggio. They tell him 'you're all right—go ahead and run on that heel.' Maybe he looks all right, but it's probably hurting him like the devil."

Hogan pushed his rehabilitation, and often overextended himself. The muscles of his legs cramped after short periods of exercise, but he did not yield in his efforts. He began slipping out of the house and trying to walk the streets. Valerie, discovering his absence, got into the car and set out to find him. When she did, he was usually waiting somewhere, his legs so cramped he could not move.

Even as Hogan followed his recovery program and people speculated on his ever playing competitive golf again, he quietly mailed his entry for the 1949 U.S. Open to be played the next month. The United States Golf Association received a confidential letter from Ben.

Hogan said he was sending his entry with the hope that he would be able to play, although he had not taken a swing of a golf club since the accident. Miracles may happen, Hogan wrote, and he asked USGA officials not to release his entry so that if were able to play it would be a surprise.

USGA officials acceded to Hogan's request for secrecy, realizing at the time that it would be a miracle and a stunning surprise if he were to play. The miracle and the surprise would come, but not so soon.

In early June Hogan was not well enough to play golf, but

did go to downtown Fort Worth to autograph his instruction book, *Power Golf*. He dedicated the book to Henry Picard, who was foremost among several professional golfers who advised and encouraged Hogan in the late 1930s.

Hogan's attorneys had filed a civil suit against Greyhound Bus Company for damages and expenses in connection with the February accident. Vital to the suit was the trial on the criminal complaint filed by the state against Alvin H. Logan, the bus driver, and the trial was scheduled for June 17 in Van Horn.

Culberson County Judge James A. Terrell presided at the trial, and a jury of six men was selected to hear the testimony and render a verdict. Terrell instructed the jury that a guilty verdict must result in a fine of "not less than $25.00 nor more than $1,000, or by imprisonment in jail for not less than one month nor more than two years, or by both fine and imprisonment."

Logan's attorney based his defense on testimony that Hogan had been driving at an excessive speed and the Cadillac had skidded into the westbound lane causing the collision. Hogan testified, "I would say my speed at the time was less than twenty miles an hour."

The jury conceded that Hogan may have been traveling sixty miles per hour but concluded that the speed of his automobile was not the cause of the accident. It ruled that Logan had been negligent as charged. The sentence was the lightest permitted by law. Total fine and court costs for Logan amounted to $127.04.

The Greyhound Bus Company and Hogan's attorneys reached an out-of-court settlement. As part of the settlement, both parties were forbidden to reveal the terms.

A sports columnist of the Los Angeles *Times* wrote without attribution that Hogan received $25,000 a year, tax-free, for life. A wire service story reported the settlement as being $150,000 plus all medical expenses. Hogan could not understand all the interest.

When an Associated Press sports editor in Texas boldly asked Hogan the terms of the settlement, he was met by eyes of gray-steel glaciality.

"I think that's my personal business, don't you?" Hogan responded in chilling tone.

As the summer of 1949 waned, Hogan realized the truth. His legs would never be the same as before the accident, especially the left one, which was damaged beyond complete repair. Resolutely, he faced the task of compensating for the condition of his legs.

In August Hogan took a regular golf club in his hands. The most encouraging aspect was that the club felt good in his hands and his hands still were strong and firm from exercise, but lacking the thick calluses developed in the years prior to the accident. He began to swing the various clubs in his backyard.

His physical condition had improved enough to allow him to travel to England in September as nonplaying captain of the United States Ryder Cup team. There, he showed that mentally he was as combative as ever, that if competition were involved, there was no "new" or "mellower" Hogan.

He raised such a fuss over the question of whether the grooves in the face of the clubs of one of the British players were scored too deeply and thus illegal that he was criticized in several quarters for making too much of an issue of it. The United States trailed after the opening team matches, and Hogan was grim as he urged his players to better performances. The United States rallied to win the Cup with a near sweep of the singles the next day.

Back home in November Hogan started hitting some golf balls, then he went to the practice area at Colonial Country Club. Seeing him there, this man who had brushed death now toiling to regain his golfing skills, people marveled at his determination and will power.

Hogan still had difficulty walking and had to wear tight athletic wrappings on both legs because of the cramps and swelling.

On Saturday, December 10, ten months and eight days after the accident, Ben Hogan played a full eighteen holes of golf at Colonial Country Club. He rode in a golf cart, however, and did so again on Sunday.

The story about the rounds in the Fort Worth *Star-Telegram* credited Hogan with scores of 71 and 72—par at Colonial was 70—and those playing with Hogan verified the tallies. Hogan said he was flattered but he had not done nearly so well— the newspaperman was merely being kind. Hogan simply did not recognize the rounds as true golf because he had ridden between shots.

Raymond Gafford, professional at Ridglea Country Club and friend of Hogan's since their caddy days together, played with Ben the two days.

After their second round, Gafford asked Hogan, "You going to L.A.?"

"I don't know, why?" Ben responded.

"You'd sure shock a lot of people," Gafford said.

Ben looked at Gafford, raised his eyebrows a little, and said, "You think so?"

Gafford could understand Hogan's attitude about riding the course in a cart, but Raymond was impressed nevertheless.

"He hit the shots," Gafford said. "I'd say he played awfully good."

The scores were irrelevant. Hogan was back playing golf, and the world of golf was excited and charged with anticipation. Hogan was encouraged but not convinced. A week later he walked and played eighteen holes, and the effort sapped his body's strength so much that he immediately went home to bed, depressed at the possibility he might never be able to recondition himself for tournament golf. He shook off the mood and was back at work on the practice tee the next day.

He believed he would need two tournaments, perhaps more, to learn if he could play championship golf again. Championship golf was his only objective. He was determined to settle for nothing less, and he was impatient to find out.

Hogan announced in mid-December that he was filing his entry for the Los Angeles Open to be played in early January 1950. Few were prepared for the news. Most of his friends thought he was forcing himself into competition too soon. Valerie knew the truth.

"Ben seemed to feel that all those people who had been encouraging him expected it," she said. "Ben didn't want to let them down."

Sponsors of the Los Angeles Open, realizing the situation, gave Hogan a graceful escape route should he be unable to compete. They invited him to be "honorary starter" of the tournament.

There may have been some question regarding his physical condition, but Hogan's response to the invitation removed any doubt about his mental readiness.

"Honorary starter, hell!" Ben snorted. "If I go out there, I'm going to play."

3

Don't ever see your superior. They may have more money, but you're just as smart./Clara Hogan, to her children, 1922.

William Ben Hogan was the third child and second son born to Clara and Chester Hogan in Dublin, Texas, a small cow town eighty-one miles southwest of Fort Worth.

His father was not a golf professional, nor a greenskeeper. The family did not live across the street from a golf course; there was no golf course in Dublin, Texas, on August 13, 1912.

Not until the next year, 1913, when Francis Ouimet, who

did live across the street from the Country Club at Brookline, Massachusetts, won the United States Open over that course did the game become nationally recognized. Ouimet became the game's first American hero. His victory removed the stigma of "rich man's sport" from golf and inspired thousands to start playing.

But by no stretch of the imagination can it be said that Francis Ouimet's influence reached into the Chester Hogan household in Dublin, Texas.

Chester was a blacksmith and a mechanic. He was skillful with his hands, a dexterity inherited by his youngest child.

The Chester Hogan family was not so desperately poor as some later accounts portrayed it. Clara Hogan recalled that at one time they owned their home, the blacksmith business, and a rent house in Dublin.

What fortunes the family had, however, turned downward in 1921 when ill health began to interrupt Chester's work. When his condition did not improve, Clara moved the family to Fort Worth in August so that her husband could see a specialist regularly. The Hogans occupied a house at 305 Hemphill Street.

Chester tried to find some work in Fort Worth but was unable to do so. In January 1922 he returned to Dublin and opened a blacksmith shop again. He returned to Fort Worth in February hoping to induce his wife to go back to Dublin with him.

Clara objected with the argument that the children should remain in their Fort Worth school until the end of the term. After an argument about the matter on the evening of Monday, February 13, Chester Hogan began to rummage in his valise in the living room of the small house. Royal Hogan asked, "Daddy, what are you going to do?"

For an answer, Chester Hogan, beset by ill health and financial worries, pulled a .38 revolver from the valise and shot himself above the heart. He died twenty-three hours later at Protestant Hospital. It was Valentine's Day.

Chester Hogan's death at thirty-seven left Clara, thirty-two, and her children—Royal, thirteen; Princess, eleven, and

Ben, nine—in impoverished circumstances. Clara moved the family to a house on East Allen Avenue.

Royal quit school and became the man of the family at thirteen. He was a bicycle delivery boy for an office supply company, sold the Fort Worth *Star-Telegram* on a downtown street corner near the Westbrook Hotel, and ran a service station part-time. He also attended school three nights a week studying bookkeeping and business management.

Little wonder that Clara Hogan described her eldest as "solid as the Rock of Gibraltar" and thought golf was a foolish waste of time compared to Royal's endeavors.

Princess and Ben worked when they could in after-school jobs. Ben became a *Star-Telegram* peddler at the Texas and Pacific Railway station, walking through the trains when they arrived. Sometimes it would take him almost all night to sell his papers. More than once Royal or a friend found Ben, his old aviator cap pulled down over his ears, curled up asleep on a waiting-room bench, his head resting on his stack of newspapers.

When Royal was fifteen, he became city sales manager of the office supply company, and the boss told him to start wearing long trousers so he would look older. Royal would own an office supply company before he reached thirty years of age.

A friend told Royal that Ben could make more money as a golf caddy than *Star-Telegram* salesman. Royal and the friend took Ben out to Glen Garden Country Club. Ben, then eleven, was hardly bigger than the golf bags he proposed to carry.

Hazing was a regular routine for new caddies, and Ben's size made him a favorite target. A hill dropped off sharply at the back of the clubhouse, and repeatedly, the other caddies threw Ben's cap, then Ben, down the hill. They once rolled him down the hill in a barrel.

Ben wearied of this routine very soon. He took a bold step to stop it by challenging two of the older, bigger caddies to fistfights. When he whipped both, the hazing ended.

Several constants in Ben Hogan's life were already evident to his boyhood friends, who called him "Bennie." They had the impression he was born with a chip on his shoulder, they recognized a keen combativeness in him, they learned he did not talk much and was a hard boy to get to know.

Ben was developing a work habit that would be an outstanding characteristic in later years. He rose well before dawn on weekends, fixed his breakfast, and trotted the seven miles from his home to Glen Garden southeast of the city. An early arrival meant the possibility of caddying two rounds at sixty-five cents each and, maybe, a ten-cent tip. Some Saturday nights in the summer he slept in one of the sand traps so he would be first in line for a job Sunday morning.

The caddies' free time was usually spent in whacking golf balls around the caddy grounds with one of the old clubs available. The clubs were right-handed, but Ben was a natural left-hander and swung the clubs that way at first. Charles (Bill) Akey, an older caddy who later became a professional golfer and club-maker, kicked Ben in the seat of the britches every time he saw the lad swinging left-handed. These reminders combined with the scarcity of left-handed clubs converted Ben into a right-hand swinger. But Hogan's golf swing through the years would feature exceptional power in his left-side body and arm action.

If the caddies were not working or hitting golf balls, they might be shooting dice, their money in baking powder cans by their knees. They had to be careful, however, because the club manager, James C. Kidd, who was called "Captain," naturally, was a stern Scotsman who did not approve of gambling, cursing, or drinking. There was a long list of offenses for which Kidd would ban a caddy from the club.

One caddy never participated in the crap games. He stood around and watched—a tall, gangling youth wearing overalls and a big straw hat to keep his fair skin from being sunburned. He was John Byron Nelson, whose family had moved from Ellis county to a farm about a mile south of Glen Garden. Nelson's parents permitted him to caddy on weekends and only after church on Sundays.

Nelson was seven months older than Hogan and about a foot taller at the time. Like most of the caddies, both were skinny as fence posts. And usually hungry.

Ben's quick mind helped him avoid losing at dice, but he

was victimized by his size in another game the caddies played. Each drove a golf ball as far as he could down the caddy grounds. The one hitting the shortest distance had to walk down and pick up all the balls and return them. Ben lost nearly every time. He resorted to practice, working to get more power into his swing and distance with the ball. Soon he was not finishing last anymore, and he never would again in a driving contest.

Years later Nelson attributed Hogan's development as a powerful hitter off the tee to that beginning on the caddy grounds. And many years later Hogan would visit that caddy grounds and realize what had been a full drive for him as a youngster was actually no more than a seven-iron shot.

The caddies dug a cup at each end of the area and played back and forth to the two holes. Ben started assembling a mixed set of clubs. When he had a dollar to spare, he went downtown to the W. T. Grant store where there was a barrel of old and odd clubs on sale for a dollar each. Most of the wooden shafts were crooked, and Ben shopped carefully, rummaging through the barrel for as long as an hour before making his selection. Rarely did he find a club with a straight shaft, but he owned some clubs—it was a start.

A member named Ed Stewart impressed Hogan with his golf, and Ben caddied for him often, studying Stewart's swing and trying to imitate it. When his mother sent Ben to the store, he usually "played" his way. He hit a golf ball from one front yard to the next, over the hedges that separated most of them. He killed much of the grass in his own front lawn practicing his swing, and his trips to the store did little to enhance the other yards in the neighborhood.

He continued to sell newspapers at a downtown street corner until Clyde Milliken, the city circulation director of the *Star-Telegram*, noted a pattern developing. If it rained, Hogan was on the job selling papers. If the sun was shining, Hogan was at Glen Garden caddying or hitting golf balls.

Milliken finally told Ben he must sell papers rain or shine. The choice was simple for the boy, and the business world lost a promising prospect. While attending Jennings Junior High School and Central High School, where he was an above-average

27

student, Ben went to parties where he occasionally sat with a girl he had met in Sunday school at Highland Park Methodist Church when both were twelve years old. Her name was Valerie Fox, and not only was she sweet and pretty, she was one of the few girls as small as Ben.

Golf was soon consuming most of Ben's spare time and attention. Clara Hogan frequently expressed her disapproval, "Why don't you utilize your spare time like your brother and get an honest job?"

Ben had not impressed very many people at Glen Garden as having any special aptitude for the game. The members considered him a good caddy. He was quiet and sharp of eye, prime requisites for the job. But Byron Nelson was the kid with golfing promise, the members thought. Already, he was established as the best shotmaker among the caddies and was a favorite of many members.

There were occasional opportunities for the caddies to demonstrate their golf. Some members would permit the caddies to play out of the bag they were carrying once they were out of sight of the clubhouse and Captain Kidd's stern gaze. There was a rule against caddies playing the course, even with members, and the penalty was banishment from the caddy force.

Byron Nelson had played some stretches in par or better figures on the course. None of the other caddies had demonstrated such skill.

For one so young Ben Hogan possessed an incredible determination. He was stubborn, and he was totally committed to golf. At age fifteen Ben started proving to people who underestimated him that they were wrong.

The chance came in the annual Christmas tournament for caddies at Glen Garden. Caddies signed up for the use of members' golf clubs; the Fort Worth *Press* sports editor, Pop Boone, came out and served as tournament chairman; and after the day's competition there were a Christmas tree, presents, and a turkey dinner.

The 1927 event was scheduled for Friday, December 23. Nelson was the favorite, but little "Bennie" Hogan startled everyone by shooting the nine holes in thirty-nine strokes, two over par. His par four on the ninth hole appeared to have clinched the title for him because Nelson needed a thirty-foot putt to tie. Nelson rolled the ball into the hole to match Hogan's score.

As they walked to the tenth tee for the play-off, Ben shook his head and told Byron, "I didn't think you could make that putt."

Both boys thought the play-off would be sudden death. And when Ben scored a four and Byron a six on the first hole, it again appeared that Hogan was the winner. Ben thought he was. But officials decided the play-off should be a full nine holes. Nelson sank an eighteen-foot putt for a par four on the ninth hole of the play-off for a score of 41 that beat Hogan by a stroke. Nelson was presented a mid-iron. Hogan as runner-up received a mashie.

In 1928 Glen Garden members decided to honor an outstanding caddy by giving him a junior membership in the club. For a boy who lived golf, this would be the ultimate possession. He could practice and play the course.

The members asked Captain Kidd to submit the name of a deserving caddy. Kidd made the nomination with these words: "Byron Nelson is the only caddy who doesn't drink, smoke, or curse. I think he should have it."

About the same time, now sixteen and no longer working in the pro shop because of that age limit, Ben went to Glen Garden, found Captain Kidd, and asked if he could practice in the caddy area. Kidd refused permission.

Ben was embittered. Nelson later won the Glen Garden junior and invitational championships, but Hogan was unable to enter those tournaments because he was not a member of any country club. He could not even practice at the course where his lifelong association with golf had begun. Many years passed before the bitterness dissipated and Ben visited Glen Garden again.

Clara Hogan's efforts to divert Ben's life to a channel other than golf continued. "I was on him again about getting an honest job," she recalled. "I asked him why he didn't get a job like Royal and go to work. 'You'll never get anywhere fooling around those golf courses,' I told him. I did not think he had much future in golf. When I finished speaking my piece, he stood there and his eyes just blazed.''

According to her, Ben said, "Momma, someday I'm gonna be the greatest golfer in the world.''

When Hogan became the world's greatest golfer, he said he could not remember ever saying those words to his mother.

Clara Hogan's surrender to her son's obstinance was displayed in tangible form. She asked Royal how much a set of golf clubs cost and he replied, "About forty dollars.''

"Here's forty dollars, then,'' she said. "Get 'em. I'm going to give them to Ben for a Christmas present.''

Golf took Ben away from school more and more until he was absent from Central High more than he was present. He did not graduate.

He continued to play in amateur tournaments and officially became a professional golfer at the age of nineteen.

His final amateur tournament was at Shreveport, Louisiana, and he did not win anything. He sold his watch to pay his caddy. Hogan hitchhiked back to Fort Worth, caught a ride in an open touring car, and it rained all the way.

His mother's prediction that he would "never get anywhere fooling around those golf courses'' was quite accurate for several years.

4

I remember Ben Hogan standing outside the Claremont Country Club at Oakland, California, in 1938, beating his fists against a brick wall.

"What happened, boy?" we other young pros asked.

"I can't go another inch," groaned Ben. He was as close to tears as that tough little guy can get. "I'm finished. Some son of a bitch stole the tires off my car."/Sam Snead, 1962

One of the marvels of sports history is that Hogan stayed with golf at all.

His play as an amateur golfer certainly did not presage any brilliant career as a professional. He had occasionally kept pace with Byron Nelson, Ralph Guldahl, Gus Moreland, and others of similar ability in the amateur tournaments. Still, there were amateurs whose names would never be well known who beat Hogan.

The Great Depression was a blight upon the land when Hogan became a professional. Those were the years, as described by Sam Snead, when you could find an ex-pro in every poorhouse. Fort Worth was a rough, tough, wide-open city, too. Once Ben and three other young men were taking a shortcut through a shallow valley running parallel to the first fairway at the Oakhurst golf course. A foursome of members had teed off and was walking down the fairway, each of the men still carrying his driver. As the young men neared the crest of the slope they saw two men step from behind a couple of large oak trees near the fairway. The two men had long-barreled forty-five revolvers called hoglegs in each hand.

The four golfers were ordered to raise their hands, and four golf clubs were quickly pointed skyward. Hogan and his three friends watched as the two robbers found money in the pockets of three of the golfers. Finding no money on the fourth, the robbers threatened to pistol-whip him. The golfer was frantically trying to indicate with his upraised driver and his eyes that there was money in the watch pocket of his pants.

The robbers finally understood and found six hundred dollars in the watch pocket. The robbers departed, and soon a car motor roared to life.

"I've got a thirty-thirty in my car," said Hogan, referring to a rifle in his Hudson roadster. "I'm gonna' go get it and go after those guys."

"Ben," said a companion, "by the time you go back to your car and get your rifle, those guys will be in Cleburne. Forget it."

Most of the men who frequented the golf courses did not use guns to fleece their victims. But a number of them around Fort Worth were considered bandits, nevertheless.

Fort Worth boasted that it was the city where the West

begins. Some knowingly added, "and where civilization ends." It was the first good-sized watering hole for the new-rich oil and cattle men from that vast stretch of West Texas. These men came to town looking for action.

Along with them came con artists, grifters, sharpies, professional gamblers, and hustlers of every type.

Gambling was illegal but flourished. Winning twenty-five dollars on a game of golf was considered big money among those scratching to keep body and soul together. They would play, as the saying went, for money, marbles, or chalk.

And there were golf matches with more money riding on the outcome than the combined prize total offered by the United States Open and Professional Golfers' Association championships. The match might pit amateur against amateur, amateur against professional, or professional against professional. To the men making the huge wagers, it made no difference—the golfers were like race horses. They soon learned which golfer's hand shook after the bet was doubled. This was not a milieu for the meek.

Some of the matches became legendary in the links lore of the Southwest. Hogan against Ray Mangrum at Dallas' Cedar Crest, Nelson versus Gus Moreland at Glen Garden were among them.

Those were tough years for Hogan. Like most other young men he did a little of everything to make a living. He worked in the oil fields. He was a mechanic, for which he had a natural aptitude. He worked for a bank. He worked for a hotel. He also learned to be a check dealer—almost overnight, once again demonstrating the marvelous hand and eye coordination and mental agility. Among his earliest golf backers was the man who owned the dice game for which he was a croupier.

Hogan was not proud of this period in his life. For a man whose sole desire was professional golf success, they were years of dissatisfaction and disillusionment. He believed he should have been on the professional golf circuit winning tournaments.

He first tried the professional circuit in January 1932. With an audacity to match his determination, he went to California with seventy-five dollars in his pocket.

Hogan tied for thirty-eighth place in the Los Angeles Open and won $8.50. He stayed on the tour until New Orleans, but then was back in Fort Worth and broke.

He had shown he could hit the long ball off the tee, but otherwise his game was very inconsistent. Hogan became an assistant to Ted Longworth, head professional at Oakhurst. As his duties would permit, he was on the practice tee working on his game.

He and a boyhood friend, Buell Matthews, who had become a professional caddy after leaving the Glen Garden ranks, had a unique con game going at Oakhurst.

If someone was watching Hogan belt out his long drives while practicing, and it was a rare day when there was not a gambling type around, Matthews would walk up. He would make the comment that he could catch the golf ball being hit by Hogan—and bare-handed.

The unlikely combination of Hogan hitting the ball so accurately and Matthews catching it bare-handed usually hooked the onlooker into a bet. It would start with Matthews catching one of Hogan's drives about 220 to 240 yards away. The wagering might escalate to Matthews' shagging seven of ten without breathing hard before the loser quit.

Matthews would later boast, "We busted everybody at Oakhurst with that one."

The following winter Hogan tested the tournament trail again. He lasted a little longer, but soon was home again, back at odd jobs and practicing.

Hogan was professional at Cleburne Country Club early in this period, before going to Oakhurst. Valerie Fox's family had moved to Cleburne, and she and Ben had occasional dates through the years after they first met as twelve-year-olds. Valerie was the daughter of Mr. and Mrs. C. M. Fox. Her father was the projectionist at the Cleburne movie theater.

It was in Cleburne that the most positive event of these years occurred for Ben. On Sunday, April 14, 1935, he and Valerie were married. Valerie had a quality rare in those days— she believed in Ben and his dream of becoming a top golfer. He needed her faith, confidence, and encouragement.

Clara Hogan remarked years later, "Valerie is the only one who can honestly say, 'I told you so.' The rest of us hoped Ben would make it, but Valerie was always sure he would."

They were a strikingly handsome couple. Valerie was a petite brunette with fawnlike dark eyes highlighting her pretty face. She was small, soft-spoken, but more eloquent and less shy than Ben.

Hogan was a good-looking man. He stood 5′ 8½″ and weighed 135 pounds. He had finely chiseled features, slate-blue eyes of burning intensity, and slightly wavy black hair. Some said he resembled, in a way, George Raft, the movie star. Hogan even took a screen test in January 1941, but was content to leave the acting to Raft and others.

Deep as her love and belief were, Valerie did not have any immediate profound effect on her husband's golf game. Their primary goal after marriage was for both to work and save money so Ben could stay on the tour for an extended period without the pressure of having to make good quickly or quit again.

Hogan qualified for the United States Open at Baltusrol, New Jersey, in 1936. He did not score low enough the first two rounds to join the seventy-six golfers qualifying to play the final thirty-six holes.

Along with such disappointments and his own frustrations, Hogan was acutely aware of his contemporaries' success. Ralph Guldahl, Nelson, and another former caddy he knew, Jimmy Demaret of Houston, had already won tournaments. Demaret won the first of his six Texas PGA titles in 1935, and Nelson won the New Jersey State Open that year. In 1936 Guldahl won the Western Open and Nelson the Metropolitan Open, both prestigious events.

By the end of 1936, Ben and Valerie had saved $1,450 and had bought a secondhand Buick for $550. Ben said to Valerie, "It's now or never."

As the months passed, it looked more and more like never. They joined the golf caravan in Canada and followed it from there to Nassau to Florida to California. The crowds bothered Ben, the travel was wearying, and the competition was tough.

Hogan found that he had not learned to concentrate, to ignore the gallery and the other golfers. He realized he must shut his mind to everything except his own game. And he continued to spend most daylight hours either on the course or on the practice tee. At night he worked on his putting stroke in his room.

In his first year on the tour, 1937, Ben did not qualify for either the Masters Tournament or the United States Open. Nelson won the Masters and Guldahl the Open. Guldahl's score of 281 established a record for the Open that lasted until 1948. The man who would break it was struggling just to make golf his livelihood—and he seemed to be losing the struggle. Either his game was erratic and he would score badly in at least one round, or his putting was terrible and he scored badly in two or three rounds.

Sam Snead was rooming next to the Hogans during a Los Angeles Open about this time. One evening he overheard an aggravated Hogan complaining about his putting.

"Would you like to know how to sink those putts?" Snead heard Valerie ask.

"You know how?" Ben responded.

"Yes, I do," said Valerie.

"Then why the hell haven't you told me? How?" Ben exclaimed.

"Just hit the ball a little closer to the hole," Valerie said.

Sam said it was the best advice he ever heard, and Hogan told the story a number of times later with the same conclusion.

When the tour reached Oakland in January 1938, the Hogans had been living on oranges for almost a month. They had only eight dollars left and were staying in the cheapest motel they could find while Ben competed in the Oakland Open. The night before the final round thieves jacked up the Buick and stole the wheels. When Hogan reached the Claremont Country Club course the next morning, he told Snead and some others he was finished; they offered sympathy but no arguments.

If Hogan had never before played golf with a set jaw, lips locked into a tight smile that was not a smile, and eyes of steely intensity, the incident at Oakland might have been the beginning of his characteristic golf course demeanor.

Hogan went out and salvaged his golfing future. He shot a final-round 69, finished second to Harry Cooper, and earned $380.

"I played harder that day than I ever played before or ever will again" was Hogan's summation of the round.

Nevertheless he did not become an instant household name. That year's Calcutta Pool at the Masters Tournament offered proof of that.

Until the United States Golf Association's successful campaign to eliminate them, Calcutta Pools were a preliminary feature of most golf tournaments, professional and amateur.

Players were sold at auction, and at events such as the Masters or Las Vegas, Nevada, the bidding could become spirited and the total pot sizable. The pool paid off by percentages to the buyers with the winning player, the runner-up, and down through perhaps the first ten in medal play. In match play, any player reaching the quarterfinals might return his buyer some portion of the pool.

Calcutta Pool night at the Masters combined the trappings of a glittering social affair with those of a thoroughbred yearling sale. The old Bon Air Hotel was usually jammed.

The 1938 Masters was the first for Hogan, and the Calcutta Pool crowd shunned him as if he were a colt foaled somewhere on the lower forty by a plow horse. So Byron Nelson, defending champion, was able to buy Hogan for one hundred dollars.

It was not a bargain even at that price. Hogan shot rounds of 75-76-78-72 for 301 and a tie for twenty-fifth place. Henry Picard won and Guldahl was second.

Nelson had long believed that Hogan was a fine golfer who was overdue, and the longer Hogan went without winning, the more it puzzled Byron.

Byron and his wife, Louise, who also had met in Sunday school, and Valerie and Ben were usually a foursome at functions during a tournament. Valerie and Louise, both popular among the tour pros and their wives, became close friends.

Nelson once had two drivers made and gave one of them to Ben. The camaraderie among all the professionals, though, was more pronounced then. It was a smaller group and closer knit. When there was dinner at the club, the pros and wives dressed up. There were no sport shirts and slacks, But the pioneers of the 1930s were not entertained, wined, and dined as were those who followed them on the tour in increasing numbers fifteen to twenty years later.

The pros of the thirties were drawn together, too, by the common tribulations of trying to eke out a living when the sport was a comparative infant. Purses were small, and winners of major championships were not automatically ushered into the plush life.

As Snead put it, ". . . with 99 percent of the pros it was the same problem of hanging on by their thumbs and praying for a break."

Hogan did not qualify for the 1938 U. S. Open. From the sidelines he saw his boyhood friend Guldahl repeat as champion. Guldahl also won his third consecutive Western Open that year.

Although Ben finished 1938 as fifteenth leading money winner on the tour, he had not won a tournament. His game was still flawed by inconsistency—the bad round continued to plague him.

In 1939, still without a victory, he was moving up to seventh place on the money-winning list. But at midyear he suffered another of those set-backs that called for a serious self-appraisal.

Hogan qualified for the U. S. Open. On this second try at the Open he made the "cut" through the first thirty-six holes with rounds of 76-74 and thus was eligible to play the final thirty-six over the Philadelphia Country Club Spring Mill course. On Saturday Ben shot 78-80 for a 72-hole total of 308 and tied for sixty-second place.

He was twenty-four strokes behind Nelson, who succeeded Guldahl as Open champion by beating Craig Wood and Denny Shute in a play-off after the trio tied with scores of 284. (This was the Open best remembered for Sam Snead's distressing experience. Needing a par five on the seventy-second hole to win, Snead took an eight.)

Nelson also replaced Guldahl as Western Open champion. Hogan's teen-age contemporaries, Nelson and Guldahl, between them now had won four Western Opens, three U. S. Opens, two Masters, and assorted other titles. Ben was still seeking his first individual triumph of any kind. He was nearly twenty-seven years old, an age when a professional golfer, or any other professional, should have a very firm idea about his future.

Yet playing in his first complete U. S. Open, Hogan finished ahead of only two other contestants over the seventy-two-hole route. At that moment in Ben Hogan's career, logic could have led to the conclusion that his name might never become much better known as a golfer than the two men he beat in the 1939 Open.

Their names were George Slingerland and Frank Gelhot.

5

Ben Hogan is the most merciless player of all the modern golfers. His temperament may derive from the rough, anguishing years of his childhood or the hostility he sensed he encountered as a young and overdetermined circuit chaser. Whatever the reason, he is the type of golfer you would describe as perpetually hungry./Gene Sarazen, 1950

Ben Hogan was starving for a tournament triumph as the 1940 tour began. The achievements of Guldahl and Nelson did not dishearten him, just the contrary. They added fuel to the fires smoldering within him until he was walking around the golf courses like a volcano on the verge of eruption.

The tail-end hook on his drives still bothered him, especially after several weeks of uninterrupted tournament play when he became weary physically, but he was controlling it better. He was pacing himself better, and he was learning—no one studied the game more, or more thoroughly. The mechanics of his game were beginning to fall into place, a result of his concentration and grueling, repetitious work.

He was now confident of his putting. He adopted an open "tripod" stance where his weight was almost entirely on his left side, with his right leg acting as a prop. He used the reverse overlapping grip with the index finger of the left hand curled over the little finger of the right hand. This permitted him to have all the fingers of the right hand on the grip. He favored the right hand in putting; in fact his stroke was mostly right-handed.

Olin Dutra, who passed seventeen players to win the 1934 U. S. Open, once said of Ben: "Hogan is one of the very few golfers I know who can concentrate for 18, 36, or 72 holes without letting up. Ben wasn't good on the greens but he made himself good. When he putts I want to turn my back, because he has developed a rather weird style. But it gets results. He is deadly on four-to-six-foot putts."

Hogan was a picture of ferocity in striking his woods and long irons. Every fiber of his being appeared to be harnessed and working together fluidly and fully when he unleashed a tee shot.

As a tour sidelight a driving contest was arranged for the Los Angeles Coliseum in 1940. A temporary tee was built on the peristyle at the east end of the mammoth stadium. The test was to determine if anyone could drive a golf ball over the wall and into the seats at the west end of the stadium. The wall separating the seats from the track and field was 250 yards from the tee.

Two players' drives cleared the wall and fell into the seats. Jimmy Thomson boomed one that was measured at 265 yards. Hogan's effort was marked at 253 yards. Thomson, acknowledged as the longest hitter on the tour, weighed seventy pounds more than Ben.

When the touring pros invaded North Carolina in March, Hogan was the second-leading money winner of the year and had finished second by a stroke to six different players in six tournaments the previous fourteen months.

He pointed out the positive aspects of the situation to Valerie. Six players had beaten him by a stroke, thus there was no *one* player who could outscore him consistently. His attitude was excellent. He felt strong physically. The volcano was about to erupt, and the fallout would make golfing history.

The North-South Open at storied Pinehurst was the first stop in North Carolina. It was a premier event annually, and a large field for the times, eighty professionals and amateurs, entered. They were to compete over the famous No. 2 course which played to a par of 36-36—72.

The tournament started on Tuesday, March 19. Hogan birdied the first two holes, three of the first four, and never looked back. He was not flawless; there were two bogeys on his card. But he shot 32-34—66—to tie the course record and take a three-stroke lead over Paul Runyan.

In the second round Hogan had only one bogey as he posted a 33-34—67. He finished with four consecutive threes, including an eagle on the 473-yard sixteenth hole. There, he blistered his drive, then rifled a three-iron second to within fifteen feet of the cup and sank the putt.

His 133 total for thirty-six holes shattered the course and tournament records for the distance and was acclaimed as a new standard for championship golf in the United States. The score also left his closest pursuers, Sam Snead and Johnny Revolta, seven shots in arrears at 140.

The final thirty-six holes on Thursday were almost a formality, but not quite. Hogan tried to play cautiously on the morning's third round, and it was not a tactic suited to his temperament or his game. He repeatedly underclubbed his irons and faltered to a 74.

Fortunately for him, Snead gained only one of the seven strokes. Hogan had lost some of his momentum, but in the afternoon he was on the pins with his irons and closed with a 70, which withstood Snead's onrushing 67 by three strokes. Nelson was third with 286.

Hogan, leading from the start, scored 277, eleven under par and cutting two strokes off the tournament record. After almost nine years of famine as a professional golfer, the work and patience and persistence were rewarded. Ben Hogan finally was a winner.

Gene Sarazen may have gotten the impression that Hogan was perpetually hungry, but he and the other touring professionals were soon to learn just how insatiable an appetite Ben really had. While still in North Carolina he quickly added Greensboro and Asheville to his conquests. It amounted to the most sensational stretch of golf in the history of the game. In less than two weeks he had won three tournaments. It had never been done before and it has never been done since.

Hogan played the 216 holes of the three tournaments thirty-four strokes under par.

He broke par on eleven of the twelve rounds.

He broke 70 on ten of the twelve rounds.

He three-putted two greens in 216 holes of tournament competition—the third hole in the second round at Asheville and the first hole in the third round.

He also won $3,400 in first-prize money for the three events, boosting his winnings to $6,438 for the first three months of 1940 and placing him No. 1 in that category.

Total prize money for twenty-seven tournaments on the 1940 Professional Golfers' Association tour was $117,000, which is smaller than the purses offered by most single events on the present-day schedule. But a person kept a great deal more of what he earned in those days, and what he kept went farther in the marketplace. Winning $3,000 in two weeks on today's tournament circuit cannot be related to what it meant to Ben Hogan in 1940.

There was no way he or anyone else was going to do an encore to North Carolina the rest of that year.

At Augusta Hogan had rounds of 73-73-69-74 for 290 and a tie for tenth place as Jimmy Demaret won with 280. In the PGA

Championship at Hershey Country Club, Hogan reached the quarterfinals.

More satisfying to Hogan and another boost to his rising morale was a dramatic improvement in the most prestigious tournament, the U. S. Open. At Canterbury Country Club in Cleveland his rounds of 70-73-69-74 beat his previous year's Open total by eighteen strokes, and the 290 tied for fifth only three back of the winner, Lawson Little.

It was the year Hogan needed. He finished as leading money winner with $10,655. He had lagged well behind Guldahl and Nelson for years, and a major championship was a goal yet to be attained. But he had started to catch up.

Hogan and Nelson were friends off the course, and when on vacation from the tour they frequently went duck hunting together in Louisiana or bird-shooting in Texas. Sometimes they were accompanied by Jimmy Demaret and Guldahl. Hunting was Hogan's favorite method of relaxation from the rigors of the tournament circuit.

But when he was on the course in competition, Hogan had no friends. Whether it was par, the course, or player, it was an enemy to be conquered. Through the 1930s he had developed a deep-rooted hatred of losing, and he drove himself to avoid the experience as frequently as possible.

He concentrated more on the practice tee before a round than most of the pros did on their rounds, and he was at that practice area before and after nearly every round. One could never tell from watching him practice whether Hogan was leading the tournament by ten strokes or trailing by ten.

He took care of himself physically, ate regularly, drank sparingly, went to bed early. But he chain-smoked, half a cigarette one after the other, during a tournament round.

"The rules and equipment are fine," he once complained. "The only thing that golfers need is more daylight. There isn't enough time during the day to practice and play to key one's game to where it should be."

"Ben Hogan is the one player I know who has the physical and mental stamina to play his best golf after expending maximum power and concentration on the practice field," Sarazen said. "It exhausts me, and most of the other professionals, just to watch Ben practice, and there are occasions on which I think that even the super-disciplined Hogan leaves his finest strokes on the practice grounds."

Hogan did not leave many there in 1941, when he repeated as leading money winner, this time with $18,358, and as the tournament player with the lowest average number of strokes per round.

He and Sarazen teamed to win the Miami Four-Ball, and Sarazen related an incident that illustrates why Herbert Warren Wind, the eminent golf writer, described Hogan as playing "with the burning frigidity of dry ice."

Hogan and Sarazen went to lunch during one of their early-round matches at Miami with an eight-up lead. Before they started out on the afternoon's concluding round Sarazen suggested to Ben that there was no need to push themselves, they might as well take it easy.

"I should say not," Hogan replied. "We ought to keep piling it on. If we can beat these guys 14 and 12, I'd like that. I want to get this match over as soon as possible anyway. I want to get back to my room and practice my putting."

His fellow professionals avoided rooming next door to Ben if they could, because in the evenings there was always a constant *thump-thump* emanating from Hogan's room as he kept putting golf balls.

In the course of his 1941 campaign Hogan established a record by finishing in the money in fifty-six consecutive tournaments. Although he moved through the year still seeking his first major championship, Hogan continued to improve his finishes in the Masters and the U. S. Open.

The attack on Pearl Harbor on December 7, 1941, and the entrance of the United States into World War II hung like a cloud over the golfers, and they began 1942 uncertain of the future.

The highlight of the 1942 campaign was the Masters Tournament. Nelson, whipping out with a 68 and a 67 the first two rounds for a record halfway score of 135, took a commanding lead. Hogan started 73-70 and was eight shots back. Ben made up five of those in the third round with a 67 to Nelson's 72, and closed the gap on the final eighteen holes with a 70 to Nelson's 72. They tied at 280.

So once more the two friends and rivals were matched in a play-off as they had first been in the 1927 caddy championship at Glen Garden when they were both fifteen. Nelson was more tense than usual, and his upset stomach caused him to vomit a few minutes before they teed off.

Hogan moved ahead by three strokes on the first five holes, then Nelson played a phenomenal stretch of golf over the Augusta National course. He was six under par on the next eight holes, including an eagle three at the eighth. That erased Hogan's lead and gave Nelson a three-shot edge, and although Hogan battled back he could not quite catch Byron. Nelson won with a three-under-par 35-34—69—to Hogan's 36-34—70.

No official award was made, but Hogan finished the 1942 schedule with the lowest average strokes per round for the third straight year and was the leading money winner again with $13,143. Nelson, second to Hogan in 1940 and third in 1941, was second again in 1942.

6

Hogan is the hardest worker I've ever seen, not only in golf but in any other sport./Robert T. (Bobby) Jones, 1944

On March 1, 1943, the mail included a notice from the Tarrant County Selective Service Board ordering Ben to report for a final physical examination and induction into the armed services on March 25.

He was sworn in as a private—he had no high school diploma—at the Dallas induction center. His physical examination report listed his health excellent and his weight at 138 pounds.

He was not missing a great deal on the tournament circuit—there was none. Nearly all the regular events had been canceled for 1943.

On April 23 Private Hogan played a war bond exhibition with Colonel C. E. Henderson, Bob Hope, and Ed Dudley, president of the Professional Golfers' Association. It was the first of several such exhibitions Hogan played.

In the early stages of World War II, however, playing golf was generally frowned upon as too frivolous a pursuit, almost unpatriotic. A man who complained about the shortage of golf balls invited scorn from his fellow citizens.

The USGA suggested that golf clubs plow up part of their roughs and plant victory gardens, but very few went that far. Most clubs were concerned with draining lakes and recovering golf balls for reprocessing.

The Army Air Corps found a different use for the Bayshore golf course in Miami. It was converted into a drill field and obstacle course for the men going through Officer Candidate School.

Hogan easily passed the entrance tests for OCS and late in the summer of 1943 was sent to Miami. He spent many hours on the golf course but he was not drilling one-iron shots. He was simply drilling.

The weary OCS candidates sang a song to the tune of "Take Me Out to the Ball Game" as they marched to the Bayshore:

> Off we go to the golf course
> We ain't gonna' play golf.
> Gone are the caddies around the place
> Gone are the balls that we once used to chase.
> For they've leveled off all the sandtraps,
> Closed up the bar and the grille.
> No, it's not for golf that we're out,
> It's a goddamn drill.

Hogan graduated from OCS and was commissioned a second lieutenant on November 13, 1943. He was assigned to Fort Worth

Army Air Field as a physical training officer and led several classes of men each day through their calisthenics.

Nelson with hemophilia and Harold (Jug) McSpaden with sinusitis had been rejected by the armed forces. When tournament golf was resumed in 1944, the two of them won so often they became known as the "Gold Dust Twins." Nelson and McSpaden had been very close friends for many years, and Nelson was the godfather of McSpaden's son.

The more Nelson did, the more Hogan seethed in the shackles of service. And Nelson did plenty. The nation was hungry for a sports hero, and Nelson satisfied that appetite.

The competition was scarce and many of the courses short and flat. But there was still par, although Nelson made it a meaningless figure in 1944 and 1945.

After ten tournaments in 1944 he was sixty under par, and he averaged 69.97 strokes for eighty-five competitive rounds that year. Nelson won six tournaments and was runner-up in the PGA Championship to Bob Hamilton. He won $37,967.69 in war bonds. Nelson was voted Athlete of the Year in the national Associated Press poll. He continued to dominate golf for most of 1945.

Hogan was separated from service in August in time for the Knoxville Open of that year and was eager to make up for lost time. There now was not much love lost between Nelson and Hogan. Their rivalry was too intense for the close friendship to survive. Nelson backers said Ben in action and word showed he resented the success Nelson had attained in the war years. Hogan backers explained that he was too combative to be a buddy to the man who stood between him and his goal.

But there remained a strong mutual respect between Nelson and Hogan, and as the years passed, their relationship became closer again. They had shared too many experiences for their friendship to become permanently estranged.

In a postwar mood of euphoria, fans looked forward to resumption of the Hogan-Nelson rivalry, and they wanted to see Snead, too, because the West Virginian had the beautiful natural swing, was a big hitter and a colorful personality.

Nelson shot 276 at Knoxville, beating Sam Byrd by ten shots and Hogan by eleven. In horse racing, that tournament might be called a "tightener" for Hogan, a conditioning outing that brought his game to sharp form.

The next week at Nashville Ben was his prewar formidable self. He led off with a 64 over the Richland course and romped home with a 265, nineteen under par and four ahead of Nelson and Johnny Bulla, who tied for second. Any doubts that may have arisen among the fans were dispelled—they were going to get their money's worth out of golf competition in the postwar era.

Nelson accumulated nineteen victories in 1945, including a streak of eleven straight. Both were records, and still are. He won $63,335.66 in war bonds, then an all-time high on the professional circuit. He also shattered Hogan's record of finishing in the money in 56 consecutive tournaments—Nelson had done it in 112 straight. He was named Athlete of the Year again in the Associated Press poll.

Hogan had a good year despite being able to compete for less than five months. He won five tournaments, tied for second in two, was third in four, and tied for third in another. He was the third money winner of 1945. But he was not going to be satisfied until he regained his ranking as No. 1. And Nelson was the man to beat for that honor.

Their rivalry, the highlight of the tour and a delight to the spectators, lasted a year. From August 1945 to August 1946 they waged a furious battle. In that period Hogan won eighteen tournaments, Nelson ten. Hogan partisans felt they had a clear-cut winner. Nelson supporters argued that their man had taken prolonged vacations from the tour and pointed to his lower average score per round as indicative of his superiority. Whatever the various prejudices, Hogan and Nelson in their resolute combat destroyed par.

Hogan once against was runner-up in the Masters, and it was agony for the man who desperately wanted to win one of the three major United States championships. He needed two putts from twelve feet above the cup on the final hole to tie Herman

Keiser. Ben three-putted. His rounds of 74-70-69-70 for 283 placed him second by a stroke, his second straight miss by that margin in the Masters.

Ben had another bitter experience in the U. S. Open at the Canterbury Club in Cleveland. After rounds of 72-68-73 he came to the seventy-second hole needing to sink a five-foot putt to tie Vic Ghezzi, Lloyd Mangrum, and Nelson for the championship. Hogan missed the putt. Mangrum, Nelson, and Ghezzi all scored 72s in the first play-off. Mangrum shot another 72 on the second eighteen while Ghezzi and Nelson carded 73s. So Hogan had to settle for fourth place.

Having missed by a putt in the Masters and the Open, Hogan set to work weeks before the PGA Championship at Portland Country Club. He practiced every hour he could. His absorption was so complete that he was more glacial than normal. Nelson, too, placed the PGA Championship at the top of his priority list. He was defending champion and announced that after the tournament he would no longer play regular tournament golf. He was going into semiretirement on his ranch at Roanoke, near Fort Worth, and would emerge only for the Masters, Ryder Cup, or other select events.

Nelson had a temperament that was kept well hidden from the public. He had thrown his share of clubs and was in more than one fistfight as tempers flared on the tour. He learned to keep the tension bottled up inside. It was his undoing. He aged well beyond his thirty-four years. He had played himself out.

Bobby Jones talked about temperament one day at Augusta: "I was always tense before I went out. I couldn't have done anything if I hadn't been. The days I didn't feel anything, I didn't score. Nelson is of the same temperament. Hogan, Hagen, Sarazen, I don't think they feel anything. They aren't built that way."

The kind of golf Hogan and Nelson had played going into the PGA Championship at Portland Golf Club in Oregon naturally led to the strong possibility they would meet in the long-anticipated head-to-head confrontation which had not occurred over the year of their postwar rivalry. Their credentials were such that when Hogan and Nelson were placed in opposite brackets, everyone looked ahead to the joyful prospect not only of their meeting, but meeting in the finals for a championship.

Nelson and Hogan kept the drama alive for three days. But Ed (Porky) Oliver spoiled the fans' anticipation with a one-up triumph over Nelson in the quarterfinals. Hogan eased past Frank Moore, five and four. And while Oliver was moving past Harold (Jug) McSpaden, six and five, in the seminfinals, Hogan was demolishing his partner and friend, Demaret, ten and nine, by playing twenty-seven holes in one hundred strokes, eleven under par.

Ben drew some criticism for his shellacking of Demaret. There were those who felt he could have shown some mercy for his friend and partner.

Demaret accepted the embarrassment with his usual good humor. Asked what was the turning point of the match, he replied, "The first tee this morning, of course." Did Hogan have much to say? Mostly, Demaret related, Ben just said "Ugh!" But occasionally he spoke a couple of words on the green. What were they? "You're away."

Through the morning's round of the finals it appeared that Hogan again was going to be denied in his quest for a first major championship. Oliver held a three-up advantage. Porky might clown around in the pretournament clinics and sometimes on a tournament round, but he could be a tough opponent. Hogan learned that in the 1941 Western Open at Phoenix, where he finished the seventy-two holes thinking he would win the tournament by three strokes. Oliver came blazing home with a 28 on the final nine to beat Ben by a stroke with 275.

This time Hogan held the hot hand. After lunch he staggered Oliver with a 30 on the front nine and by the thirty-first hole of the match had forged a five-up edge. Their drives on the thirty-first fairway were so evenly matched that the referee, Ed Dudley, tossed a coin to determine which player would hit first. Hogan won the toss and struck his approach shot to within three feet of the pin to end the match, six and four.

His first major title tucked away, Hogan added four more tour victories before the year ended. He won the Golden State Invitational, the Dallas Invitational, the Winnipeg, Canada, Open and the North and South Open. He won thirteen tournaments and was the leading money winner with $42,556.16.

The postwar popularity of golf filled the year with tournaments, and the PGA had more sponsors wanting tournament dates than could be granted. Prize money increased proportionately.

Hogan had reestablished his supremacy and no longer had to contend with Nelson, but his hold on the position was disputed by Demaret. Hogan did not underestimate Demaret—they had played together too often for that—but generally the genial man from Houston was not fully appreciated for his golfing ability. Primarily, that was because of his flamboyant behavior and dress. He wore clothes that were outrageous, and he was gregarious where Hogan was silent and withdrawn.

Demaret chatted with the fans, unreeled quips like Bob Hope and played exceptionally fine golf. He never won the Open or the PGA but he was a three-time champion of the Masters. And his second Masters was won in 1947, when he knocked Hogan off the perch as king of the professional golfing hill.

Demaret scored 281 in that Masters. Nelson and Stranahan, the amateur, had 283s, and Hogan was fourth at 284 on rounds of 75-68-71-70. In the 1947 U. S. Open, Hogan could do no better than 289 with rounds of 70-75-70-74, tying for sixth behind Lew Worsham and Sam Snead at 282. Worsham won the play-off at St. Louis Country Club, 69 to 70.

And, defending his PGA Championship at Plum Hollow Country Club in Detroit, Hogan was unceremoniously ushered to the sidelines in the first round by Toney Penna, three and one.

There were brighter moments in the 1947 campaign. Hogan, who had won the L. A. Open in 1942 at Hillcrest by beating Thomson in a play-off, started with another victory in that tournament, which had been moved to Riviera. Ben opened with a 70, then tied the course record with a 33-33—66—for a four-stroke lead over Penna after thirty-six holes. Hogan finished with a pair of 72s for 280, which clipped a shot off the tournament record of 281 set by Johnny Bulla in 1941.

There was growing agitation among the touring professionals for more control over the tournament circuit. The Professional Golfers' Association approved sponsors, dates, purses, and players. The PGA ran the circuit through a tournament director, who was Fred Corcoran in 1947 when the tour moved from Los Angeles to the Monterey Peninsula for the Bing Crosby Invitational.

The squabble erupted openly there, when two seven-hour meetings of a players' committee headed by Hogan were held. Little progress was made in the meetings, and after Hogan resigned as chairman, PGA president Ed Dudley considered the committee disbanded.

Dick Metz, a veteran player on the tour, and Corcoran had been feuding over the issue for some time. And on Friday evening at Del Monte, Metz punched Corcoran in the mouth and knocked him down. Corcoran threatened to sue, but did not. Metz later was suspended from playing the Phoenix and Tucson tournaments.

In the pro-amateur preceding the Phoenix Open Hogan broke the driver he had been using for thirteen years. At the sixteenth hole he noticed the shaft was sprung. He tried to straighten it and the club fell apart. Hogan used a fourteen-ounce driver that was forty-three inches long. For a long time Hogan had been looking for another driver which felt as good to him, but he would look for years afterward before getting one that completely satisfied him.

"The only comparison I can make of the difference between golf clubs is to say that playing with a new club is something like breaking in a new pair of shoes," said Hogan. "However, I have found it a lot easier to find a new pair of shoes that I like than I have to find a new driver."

Hogan cited the experience of Bobby Jones in stressing the importance of clubs that feel "right." Jones's clubs were hickory-shafted, and he had assembled his set one by one over the years. Upon Jones's retirement, the clubs were tested scientifically for center of gravity, moments of inertia, and the like. All the clubs were found to be a perfect match with the exception of the mashie niblick, the eight-iron of today.

"I always had trouble with that club," Jones commented.

Although playing with a different driver, Hogan repeated as Phoenix Open champion.

In the Jacksonville Open that year Hogan suffered one of the more embarrassing moments of his career, but also displayed the strength of his character.

On the sixth hole, a par three of only 140 yards, Hogan dumped his tee shot into the pond fronting the green. Four times he slashed at the ball trying to move it from the water to dry land. He then lifted the ball and dropped it. He was lying six.

Hogan flubbed the pitch shot, and the ball plopped into the water again. He lifted and dropped and was lying eight. This time he made it to the green with his ninth stroke. He two-putted for an eleven. It was a grimmer-than-usual Hogan who walked off that sixth green. And he birdied the seventh hole.

Demaret added the St. Petersburg, Tucson, and Miami titles to his Masters and the two Four-Ball triumphs and was the leading money winner of 1947 with $27,936.83. Hogan finished third. He won $25,000 and complained that his expenses for the year were $20,000.

Demaret also had the lowest average number of strokes per tournament round, 69.80, and won the Vardon Trophy from Ben, who averaged 69.84 strokes per round.

Although toppled from the top spot, the Hogan of the period 1940–47 was a fiery and fierce golfer. He generated amazing velocity of the club head at impact and with his tee shots propelled the ball a prodigious distance for a man his size. The roll of the ball after the tail-end hook, though, left Hogan somewhat uncertain at times just where his drives might wind up.

He had perfect timing and exchange of weight, and he waited longer than anyone before uncocking his wrists on his downswing. After Nelson's retirement, Hogan was supreme in ability to hit the long irons.

Whatever the iron, Hogan did not aim simply for the green or a certain space on the green. He bore in on the pin itself. He thought in terms of perfection and nothing less on every shot. Valerie's admonition to get the ball closer to the hole so he could make the putts may have had nothing to do with it, but he was following her advice. His objective on every approach was to put his ball inside those of his playing partners.

Whether Hogan had said at sixteen years of age that he was going to become the greatest golfer in the world did not matter as 1947 came to a close. That definitely was his intention now, and to earn that recognition he realized he had to win some more major championships.

His success and golfing excellence thus far would have satisfied most people, but not Hogan. In the privacy of the practice tee at Colonial when he was not on the tour he had begun experimenting with a change in his grip and alteration of his swing.

When they saw the result, many of his fellow professionals could not understand why he had tampered with his game. How could the best get better? Hogan, as usual, knew what he was doing.

7

It would not be amiss to add that the superlative game he ultimately developed depended at least as much on the tireless thinking he put in over the years as it did on his tireless practicing./Herbert Warren Wind, 1957

Hogan was a classic case of the mind mastering the matter. If he required his body to react or respond in some fashion foreign to its native ability, he either willed it or studied and worked on it until the body performed as he desired.

Herbert Warren Wind collaborated with Hogan on an instruction series entitled "The Modern Fundamentals of Golf." In a preface to the final segment of that series reprinted in his book *The Realm of Sport*, Wind wrote:

Ben has a truly remarkable mind. At its core, it is the mind of a scientist. In testing the efficacy of a theory or an idea, for example, he can, upon reaching a junction in the road where two alternatives present themselves, start down one fork and make his way patiently along as he probes the many secondary and tertiary side roads, reach definite conclusions about the soundness of what he discovers at the end of the road, and, finally, either incorporate those new facts into his previous knowledge, or, rejecting the whole journey as impractical, retrace his steps without confusion back to the original junction in his investigations and set out calmly down the other fork to see what that offers.

"Well, I think anyone can do anything he wants to do if he wants to study or work hard enough," Hogan once said. "I really believe that. And relating to golf, I think, if you study and work hard enough, you can do almost anything you want to do with a golf ball in the air."

Hogan wanted to control the golf ball as completely as it was humanly possible. By 1947 he was convinced that the golfer cannot possibly control the ball once it lands and starts rolling in the fairway or on the putting surface.

"Because you don't know what is going to happen," he said. "If all putting surfaces were identical, like a billiard table, for instance, then you could control that. And you can control a golf ball in the air but not on the ground. You are subject to too many undulations and grass changes and things like that. It's utterly impossible. It could change by the hour."

Hogan decided putting was mostly intuitive in determining how hard to hit the ball or where to aim. But he believed he could do something about controlling the ball from tee to green and that was to eliminate the hook on his tee shots.

"I was a terrible hooker. I was just awful," he recounted. "I couldn't keep the ball fairly straight. And I couldn't fade one at the time, unless purely by accident. So I thought, if I'm going to be in this business, I had better stop this because if you get a sharp dogleg to the right with a lot of trees on the right, I might as well go to American Airlines and get a ticket and go somewhere else, just because I couldn't play it."

The ball rolls upon hitting the ground at the end of a hook because of the overspin on it. The hook thus is a boon to the golfer more interested in maximum flight and roll for distance. But the roll of the ball is beyond the golfer's control. Hogan was more concerned with having the ball land and stay in the vicinity of the fairway he had selected, usually having taken into account the troubles on the particular fairway and the position that would be most advantageous for making his second shot to the green.

The faded tee shot, some call it a delicately manipulated slice, coming off the slightly open club face, normally will hit and stop, rolling very little.

The mechanics of the swing and grip bringing the club face into the ball properly for a faded shot time after time are intricate, and must be finely tuned to achieve consistency. There is only a minute margin for error.

That Hogan mastered the adjusted grip and swing was not surprising to those who knew him. His concentration was illustrated once when he was playing a round with George Fazio. Hogan was keeping Fazio's scorecard. George holed out a three-iron second shot for an eagle deuce on a par-four hole. At the end of the round, Hogan, filling out Fazio's card, marked a three for the hole.

"Ben," cried Fazio, looking over Hogan's shoulder, "I made a two at that hole."

Hogan looked up somewhat blankly and said, "Aw, you're crazy."

Ben, if he had seen the shot at all, did not remember it

because of his close attention to his own game.

Valerie Hogan came to believe Ben had a photographic mind, and his ability to memorize courses, whether walking them tee to green or backward, would seem to support her.

Gardner Dickinson majored in clinical psychology at Louisiana State University before graduating and joining the professional golf circuit. Dickinson was the first, but not the last, of the young professional imitators of Hogan. Dickinson tried to swing like Hogan and dressed like him, right up the white billed cap.

He did not, as some contestants did in the Pan-American Open in Mexico City one year, try to hit his ball into the divots Hogan had taken on a round.

Dickinson liked to "test" his fellow professionals by injecting into conversations questions from the Weschsler-Bellevue International Scale measuring the intelligence quotient. He once asked Hogan if he would submit to the entire test, and Hogan replied, "No indeed."

But occasionally Dickinson, who became Hogan's assistant at the Tamarisk Country Club in Palm Springs, would sneak a question in on Ben.

There were questions such as if you were walking along the sidewalk and found a letter that was sealed, addressed, and stamped, what would you do?

"Why," Hogan replied indignantly, "I'd mail the goddamn thing!"

"That was the correct answer," Dickinson said, "but it was amazing how many missed it."

The Apocrypha refers to various writings falsely attributed to biblical characters or kept out of the New Testament as not genuine. Once Dickinson managed to ask Hogan what "Apocrypha" meant.

"I was flabbergasted that he knew," said Dickinson. Dickinson eventually concluded that Hogan had an IQ of 170 to 172. Dickinson and perhaps most others did not realize that Hogan read a great deal. For the man who did not finish high school, reading was the avenue to self-education. And Hogan had the mind to absorb and retain what he read or saw.

He learned the value of the waggle of the club from watching Johnny Revolta and talking to him in the early 1930s. He adopted Revolta's habit of modifying his waggle to suit a particular shot. Hogan studied newsreel movies of the best golfers in the mid-1930s to develop the correct hip-turn action.

Worried about the unreliability of his backswing, he began to investigate the plane seriously. In his hotel or motel room he studied the backswing plane night after night in a mirror, trying to memorize it so well that he would instinctively swing back the same way each time.

Whatever the endeavor, Hogan applied himself thoroughly. Years later he decided to learn to dance. He described himself as having two left feet when he started. He took lessons at a professional studio in Fort Worth and practiced the various steps in front of a mirror at home. After completing the course, Ben dazzled onlookers and his partners with his dancing. He was especially fond of the Latin-American routines.

Once, Bobby Locke of South Africa declined an invitation to the Colonial tournament in Fort Worth. "What's wrong with him?" Jimmy Thomson asked. "He went to New York to see a specialist, he said," was the reply. "He should come down here and see a specialist," Thomson exclaimed. "Hogan!"

Many of the pros shared Joe Conrad's sentiment. Conrad, then state amateur champion of Texas, went out to the practice tee one day with this statement, "I'm gonna' go hit a few, then go watch Hogan and see how it oughta be done."

Ernie Vossler, a young Fort Worth professional making his first appearance at the Masters, arrived at the clubhouse and asked the attendant to give him the foot locker next to Hogan. His strategy paid off.

Before one practice round, Hogan sat down to change into his golf shoes and Vossler was there. For twenty minutes Hogan imparted information about the Augusta National course—how to play certain holes in certain conditions, when to play for the pin and when to play for only the green, which side of the fairway was usually best. Hogan knew every detail of every fairway and green. Vossler would have needed to play numerous rounds to approach a similar knowledge of the course.

Tommy Bolt described the effect Hogan had on him. "I went there and played with Ben nine or ten days, and he almost had me winning the Open. He can straighten me out better than anybody. He can help me more mentally. He knows more golf than any other five men."

When Hogan was not demonstrating that knowledge on various courses, he was doing so in conversation. He did not believe a golfer ever hit the ball straight, except by accident. He said the ball goes either left or right. This evolved into a tee shot theory Hogan followed.

"I think you are better off trying to move it one way or the other, or at least try to—and making it go that way," he said. "You decrease your margin of error all the time. For instance, if you take a thirty-yard fairway and work it down the left side, you've got thirty yards to work with. But if you try to aim down the middle of the fairway, you have only fifteen yards to work with.

"It's going one way or the other and you're going to get in the rough. And the green the same way. Everybody should do something so that they can control the ball. Everybody shouldn't try to fade. They should control the ball, whether it's a hook or fade or top or sky or whatever they want to do, and when they can do the same thing every time, then you can judge distance."

Hogan thought that hitting a shot thirty feet long or thirty feet short was as bad as hitting one to right or left by the same distance. He did not criticize players when they began stepping off yardage, but he also did not agree with the trend.

"I just think it's part of the game to judge the distance," he said. "I get a great bang out of being able to look up there and say, 'That looks like a five-iron shot, but I want to lay off of it a little bit,' or 'I want to give a little bit more gas.' Personally, I get self-satisfaction out of doing that. I don't want to know the distance in the first place. If someone told me it was 167 yards, I couldn't tell you what club I'd use. I wouldn't have a clue. I think you have to visualize the shot and see the ball in the air and what's going to happen to it and where the pin is cut and where you're going to try to land it.

"It would take me a year to practice and go measure my shots to find out how far I hit a four-iron or a five-iron. I can't tell you. Lie has a lot to do with it. Wind conditions, weather conditions, humidity—everything, you have to take into consideration. If you tell me it's 167 yards, then you have to tell me how strong the wind is blowing and from what direction and if there is any humidity and if it's damp or bright shiny day with no humidity—before I can possibly come up with some kind of club for you."

On the practice tee, or on the course, other golfers went through the same motions, the same preparations, as Hogan. But Ben always left the impression that he actually knew why he was doing certain things and was really thinking about the next shot. Once, in the practice area at Colonial, a club member wondered aloud why Hogan was working so long with one particular club.

"Because I hit this club three times a round on the next course we play," answered Ben.

"Golfers who should be better than they are in tournaments miss because they don't organize their faculties," he said another time. "You just can't go out and start whacking."

He was never satisfied with his game and enjoyed experimenting with the results of hitting a ball different ways. If he discovered any ingredient that he thought would improve his golf, he worked to incorporate that.

"And that's one of the great rewards of golf, I think," he remarked. "Learning. I've seen some people play terrific golf, but they didn't know anything about it. And you see their names in the paper for two years, and then they drop out, because they weren't schooled in how to propel this club, and what was happening all the time, and why. I've gotten just great satisfaction—as much as or more than anybody—in learning how to swing a golf club and what is going to happen when you swing it this way or that way. It's so simple it's pitiful, but it takes a long time to learn."

"Simple" is not how he described it on another occasion.

"There's nine jillion things to learn," said Hogan. "If I knew somebody who knew everything there is to know about the golf swing, I'd try my doggonedest to get to him. I don't think anyone knows all there is to know about the golf swing, and I don't think anyone will ever know. It is a very complex thing. Some days you react differently, your muscles and your eyes change from day to day. Even a driving machine won't react the same on a cold day as on a warm day. It's utterly impossible. Everything changes. There are so many things I don't know about golf, you could fill a room with them. I don't know them all, and if I did, I wouldn't enjoy practicing. I like to practice and fiddle around and prove or disprove things. I'm a very curious person, and I enjoy that. And if I knew it all, I wouldn't have any more enjoyment."

Hogan thought stupidity could be eliminated from tee to green but his solution to the woes of putting was to abolish the greens. He suggested hitting the required strokes from the tee and down the fairway, but a funnel would replace the greens. After the approach shot hit the funnel the ball would roll out onto the next tee. He contended, and he was not being all that facetious about it, that golf was two different games—that from tee to green and that on the green.

Of course, this came later in his career when age and the cumulative years of tournament pressure had taken their toll on his nerves and putting stroke.

"I used to get letters about my putting," he said, "and I suppose I've gotten a room full—about how to putt and how to improve my putting. Oddly enough, they are all different. But I got one that struck me one time.

"I can't recall the fellow's name at the moment, but he had won all the championships in trap and skeet shooting. He was a national champion two years in a row. He got to where he couldn't pull the trigger. So he started shooting left-handed, and by golly, after a year and a half, he won the national championship shooting left-handed. And then I got one from a violin player. Now, violin players get to where they can't pull the bow. And it got to the same place with me in putting, you know.

"I got to where I couldn't get the putter back. I could get it through if I could ever get it back, but I couldn't get it back! I would just stand there and shake, and it wouldn't move. And people would say, 'Oh, for crissake, hit it!' I was saying to myself, 'For crissake, hit it!'

"I suppose it's a nerve thing, I don't know what it is. But it happens to some people. I think Sam [Snead] and all of us have a little touch of it from time to time as we get older. Your nerves won't hold still for you. And as a result, you are a terrible putter."

Hogan's analyses of the game through the years led him to the realization that golf is a game of mistakes. He did not think any golfer hit more than one or two shots perfectly over eighteen holes. A mistake, in his mind, was a shot that would not have been any good if it were hit perfectly and the player had anticipated all the other factors such as wind conditions and bounce of the ball.

Along with that realization came a gradual infusion of self-confidence.

"In the seasons before the war," he described it, "as I learned more and more about the golf swing and how to play golf, I enjoyed increasing success on the tournament circuit. Nevertheless, I never felt genuinely confident about my game until 1946. Up to that year, while I knew once I was on the course and playing well that I had the stuff that day to make a good showing, before a round I had no idea whether I'd be 69 or 79.

"I felt my game might suddenly go sour on any given morning. I had no assurance that if I was a little off my best form I could still produce a respectable round. My friends on the tour used to tell me that I was silly to worry, that I had a grooved swing and had every reason to have confidence in it. But my self-doubting never stopped. Regardless of how well I was going, I was still concerned about the next day and the next.

"In 1946 my attitude suddenly changed. I honestly began to feel that I could count on playing fairly well each time I went out, that there was no practical reason for me to feel I might suddenly 'lose it all.' I would guess that what lay behind my new confidence was this: I had stopped trying to do a great many difficult things perfectly because it had become clear in my mind that this ambitious overthoroughness was neither possible nor advisable, or even necessary."

Hogan strived for perfection but had learned to live with imperfections. He stressed the grooving of fundamental movements that were basically controllable. Thus, whether he happened to be sharp or not so sharp on a given morning, he thought he could still play creditably. With this attitude came a more consistent, stable game and scoring.

Hogan was not above gamesmanship when competing. Roy Stone, a professional caddy, worked for Hogan. "I'll tell you how Hogan foxes them," Stone said. "If he has a three-iron to the green, he'll take a two-iron and cut it in there. The other players watch and take a two-iron and they'll go over the green."

Stone said Hogan never asked for advice on what club to use but might inquire as to his opinion on whether an iron would be enough on a long shot.

When Hogan first appeared with his fade, he refused to answer questions as to how he had accomplished it. He said it was a secret he had discovered and he would not even tell Valerie the secret.

Trying to guess what he had done, or was doing, to effect a fade became a favorite game in nineteenth holes around the country. *Life* magazine invited six professionals to offer their suggestions. Gene Sarazen came the closest to the truth when he attributed the result to an alteration of the grip.

One golf writer in New York said it was a twenty-minute warm-up routine that Ben undertook after getting out of bed in the mornings. Byron Nelson retorted that never mind the routine, Hogan's secret was driving and short putting. Another pro said his secret was an eight-letter word starting with "p" and ending with "e,"—practice.

Hogan incorporated pronation with two other adjustments in the switch from a hooking swing to one resulting in a fade. Pronation, the turning of the hand palm down toward the body, rolled his hands on the backswing and opened the club face. He placed the left thumb down the center of the shaft and he locked his left wrist at the top of his backswing so that it could not roll back over as he brought the club head back down and through the ball. This helped him prevent a closed club face and the resultant hook.

Ben, in revealing what he had done, cautioned against adoption by bad golfers and said, "I doubt if it will be worth a doggone to the weekend duffer."

Ben's swing, when it was at its powerful, rhythmic best, had a certain beauty. But it would never be compared with Snead's for natural grace. This did not bother Hogan.

"Weight and size have nothing to do with it," Hogan said. "I want a functional golf swing. The primary purpose in a tourney is to shoot the lowest score, not have the prettiest swing."

Snead doubted that the change helped Hogan. Sam told about the 1949 Masters. Hogan was fading the ball in a practice round with Henry Picard. The day before, Picard had watched Snead reach the green in two strokes on the par-five thirteenth and fifteenth holes by hitting hard and straightaway.

"Ben," said Picard, "you'll have trouble beating Sam, because you're giving away too much distance. He'll be on in two against your three on the par fives, and over four rounds you can't spot him that much."

Snead won that Masters, his first.

"I always thought that Ben was a greater golfer on days when he let himself go off the tee with a draw at the tail end," Snead remarked.

Hogan's record in the years ahead became a strong argument against Snead's reasoning. Undoubtedly, the change contributed to Hogan rising from the ranks of great golfers to become a great champion as well.

8

The people are tired of just one or two names in the headlines. They don't want this cut and dried stuff. Sure, stronger competition will mean I'll have more trouble getting the big money but it will mean more money in the long run. A wider range of competition will mean more tournaments./Ben Hogan, 1947

Ben Hogan was doing very little to encourage his present or potential competition. Since 1946 he had been the man to beat on the professional tour. It was Hogan against the field at every tournament he played.

Finishing behind Demaret in money winning and the Vardon Trophy stroke race in 1947 tarnished Hogan's stature as the No. 1 golfer of the period. As 1948 began he set out to reclaim that ranking and in a manner that would leave no doubts.

The Los Angeles Open was to be played again at Riviera Country Club, where Hogan had won the event in 1947 with a record score of 280. The course also was to be the site of the 1948 U.S. Open, which would be contested in the West for the first time since its inauguration in 1894.

Riveria was approximately 7,000 yards long. It lay hard by the Pacific north of Santa Monica, and the greens were devilishly difficult. Fog might roll in at any time and obscure the landscape. Par was a severe 35-36—71.

In the final round, Hogan was home in 36 for a 67 and won the tournament with a 72-hole total of 275, which eclipsed by five strokes his record of 280 the previous year. Lloyd Mangrum was second at 279. Hogan attributed his score to the fast course and his approaches to the greens. The fairway position he was now attaining with his fade off the tee may have contributed to his ability to strike the approach shots so closely to the holes.

"My putting wasn't anything extra," he said. "It's been off for some time. But I was playing to the greens as well as I ever have."

Curiously perhaps, for a man who played so much golf and continually peppered the pin for years with his iron shots, Hogan had only four holes in one. Two were in tournaments at Spokane, Washington, and San Antonio, but neither figured in a winning score. Many so-called duffers have had more aces than Hogan.

The pros departed, while behind them in Los Angeles were those ready to concede the U. S. Open in June to Hogan. The Riviera course had become known as "Hogan's Alley."

Having failed to threaten in the Masters and having been dumped in the first round of the tournament in 1947, Hogan was more determined than usual to take the PGA title, second of the major championships on the schedule, held on the par 71 Norwood Hills Country Club course in St. Louis.

His semifinal foe, as in 1946, was friend James Newton Demaret. This time there would be no rout. Hogan forged a three-up edge in the morning, but after lunch Demaret twice got even. Then Hogan won the thirty-third and thirty-fourth holes and halved the thirty-fifth to win, two and one.

Reaching the finals in the opposite bracket was Mike Turnesa, a club professional who seldom competed in tour tournaments. Observers termed the final a mismatch. Hogan shot a 65 on the morning round and was ahead, four up. He held it through the first nine of the afternoon's eighteen holes, then won the twenty-eighth, twenty-ninth, and thirtieth holes to capture his second PGA Championship, seven and six. Hogan was nine under par for the thirty holes and thirty-five under par for the 213 holes he had played in the qualifying rounds and six matches.

Hogan now possessed his second major golf crown. He considered it only a beginning, but he announced that he would not play in the PGA Championship again. He made the statement when he was exhausted mentally and physically from the effort of the seven days at St. Louis. When he arrived in Fort Worth for the Colonial National Invitation, he said he had been quoted correctly but was now feeling better.

"I still think the tournament is too long, but they can't do anything about it," he remarked. "I may try again next year."

Fate had a way of making some of Hogan's statements prophetic. He would never again play in the PGA so long as it remained match play and required the contestants to compete at thirty-six holes a day for five days to win it. It would not be because Hogan scorned the tournament, rather that he would be physically inadequate to such an undertaking because of his auto accident injuries.

Hogan was superb at match play, whether on an individual or a partnership basis. He not only had the golfing skills, his mental attitude was ideally suited to man-to-man tests. Yet he did not like match play.

"You can be out on the course shooting a 67 and lose,"

he explained, "while someone else may be shooting a 75 and winning. You are out of the tournament and he is still in it with a chance to win."

Ben skipped the Albuquerque Open, which Demaret won, and took the train to Los Angeles to prepare for the U. S. Open at Riviera. This was the one title he wanted more than all others.

"Adequate preparation and knowledge of the course are essential," he later said of his pattern of appearing on the scene of major tournaments well in advance. "It really isn't fair to play in a Championship without proper practice. I have to learn the course thoroughly. But if you prepare properly, the actual Championship becomes almost incidental. It's the preparation that counts."

Charles Curtis, then golf writer for the Los Angeles *Times,* was a convert from Hogan's two L.A. Open triumphs at Riviera. And Hogan enjoyed a personal popularity in the area that generally was not true elsewhere. Curtis, who for all of his knowledge of golf and excellence in reporting suffered the abominable affliction of many in referring to Ben as "Bantam," wrote: "Bantam Ben Hogan's golfing foes had better take to cover." Curtis picked Hogan to win the Open with a score of 283. His only error was one of overcaution.

But neither Curtis nor any other observer anticipated that anyone in the field would come close to Hogan's 275 in the L.A. Open. The USGA had lengthened Riviera to 7,020 yards, longest course the Open had ever been played upon (Colonial was 7,005 yards in 1941), and had been typically diabolical in toughening up the layout by narrowing the fairways, letting the rough grow, and adding sand traps here and there.

One day a call came to the caddy pen for someone to shag balls for a contestant. Virgil Claywood was the only volunteer. Claywood reached the area where he was to meet the golfer and discovered the man was Ben Hogan.

"Gosh, I'd never even seen him before," Claywood said. Claywood, then seventeen years old, was studying at Los Angeles City College to be an operatic tenor. He caddied when he could to earn money to help pay his living expenses.

Caddying for Hogan in the practice area could be classified as a nonathletic endeavor. Usually, the greatest amount of movement required was when Ben changed clubs and motioned the caddy to retreat ten or so yards. Otherwise, on most of the irons, the caddy could stand in one spot and simply open the pocket of his apron and let the ball drop into it. Hogan was that accurate.

After the first practice session, Ben asked Claywood if he would like to caddy for him in the tournament. The young man eagerly accepted.

A writer asked Hogan the day before the Open got under way how long he intended to play tournament golf.

"As long as I can keep my keenness for the game and the will to win," Hogan replied. "I want to play for a long time because of my love for the game and the competition it affords."

The world also was aware now of the change from a hook to a fade which Hogan had made. The writers asked him about it.

"I have adopted a swing which causes the ball to fade slightly to the right as compared to the loathsome hook that used to haunt me," he answered. "I find it less exhausting. I first used it last September in the World International at Chicago [which he won]. I'm satisfied I made a wise move."

He reiterated that he had not even told Valerie what he had done to alter his swing. He definitely had reason to be satisfied with his decision to change.

Ben's fifty-four-hole total of 207 was a U. S. Open record by four strokes and propelled him into a two-shot lead over Demaret, who also had a third-round 68. Hogan, per his custom, now was playing the course and Demaret the final round.

Demaret, ahead of Hogan, closed with a 69 and was home with a 278, three strokes under Guldahl's 1937 record. Demaret's second shot on the first hole of the fourth round was struck too strongly and bounced over the green. The crowd parted to let the ball roll beyond the green. When Demaret walked up, he asked, "Aren't there any Texans in this crowd?"

Hogan birdied the first hole for the seventh consecutive time dating back to the second round of the L.A. Open in January as he started his fourth tour of the tournament. He birdied the fifth and was out again in thirty-three strokes. It was by then only a matter of keeping track of Demaret. When Hogan rolled home a fifteen-foot putt for a birdie at the tenth, he foreclosed on the field.

"That birdie of mine at the tenth seemed awfully good," Hogan said.

He took a bogey five at the fifteenth but matched par for the nine with a 36, and his 69 preserved the two-stroke margin over Demaret. Hogan won his first U. S. Open and beat the previous record for seventy-two holes by five strokes with a 276. He had come within one swing of the total he posted in the L.A. Open.

Hogan three-putted only one green in the tournament, when he took the bogey five on the fifteenth, or sixty-ninth, hole.

"I guess the ability to read the greens has been my best asset at Riviera," he said.

He was the first golfer since Sarazen in 1922 to win the PGA and Open the same year.

Hogan was asked if he might enter the British Open. "It's too late to get a reservation on a ship," he said, "and I'm not going to fly."

Hogan paid young Claywood $150, his standard amount when he won a tournament. A writer inquired of Claywood if Hogan ever sought his advice on clubs or distance in the seventy-two holes.

"Oh, no," said Claywood, "Mr. Hogan is entirely self-sufficient on a golf course."

Hogan remained in Los Angeles to make a film short and did not defend his Chicago Victory Open title the next week. But the remainder of the year was not the anticlimax it might well have been. Ben went on to win the Western Open by thrashing Ed (Porky) Oliver, 64–73, in a play-off after they had tied at 281 over the Brookfield course in Buffalo, New York.

After his course-record 64, which included seven birdies and an eagle, the committee asked Ben to say a few words at the presentation of the trophy. Ben seemed reluctant, and the story goes that a friend got up and said, "I travel with Ben Hogan quite a lot and he has a set speech for these occasions. It goes something like this: 'Thanks for the check.' "

It was in Hogan's blistering 1948 that Demaret and Cary Middlecoff began referring to him as "The Hawk," or just "Hawk." The two of them used the nickname more than other golfers generally—some credit Demaret with originating the term, others think Middlecoff did so.

Hogan was the leading money winner with $32,112. He regained the Vardon Trophy with an average number of strokes per round of 69.3. And he was voted the PGA Player of the Year.

Hogan's status as the finest golfer was secure. Unlike Guldahl, who shrugged off his decline with the comment "After winning, what else is there?" Hogan planned to work hard, improve his game, continue winning, and stay on top.

He and Valerie went home to Fort Worth and in December moved into their first house, a Colonial-style structure at 24 Valley Ridge Road. The rooms were not all furnished, but they celebrated Christmas of 1948 there. Two days later they drove their new Cadillac west toward Los Angeles. Hogan was going to defend his title in the L.A. Open and play in at least three other tournaments before they returned home.

On the eve of that L.A. Open, a drawing of Hogan by Boris Chaliapin was on the cover of the January 10 issue of *Time* magazine, and he was the subject of the feature story entitled "Little Ice Water."

"Hogan had no intention of relaxing," the *Time* story included. "1948's laurels are no good in 1949."

The correspondent quoted Riviera caddy Clyde Starr: "It takes him [Hogan] three hours to go nine holes in practice. He'll say, 'Here, drop fifteen balls in this sand trap here.' Then he'll blast every one of them out. If he's not satisfied, he'll blast another fifteen. He'll even memorize the grain of the grass. He'll putt 'til hell won't have it."

Someone asked Hogan if he ever relaxed on the course.

"Relax?" he exclaimed. "How can anybody relax and play golf? You have to grip the club, don't you?"

The *Time* article quoted one pro, without naming him, as saying, "It's no fun to play with Hogan. He's so good and so mechanically perfect that he seems inhuman. You get kind of uneasy and start to flub your shots."

And another pro, also unnamed by *Time*, said at the Montebello Open, "Look at that Mangrum. Steady as a rock out there. He even grins once in a while. But if Hogan were in this tournament, you'd see Lloyd shake when he lit a cigarette. I'm telling you, the guy's got ulcers, and Ben Hogan gave them to him."

This was unfair to Mangrum, who was about as unflappable as one could be on the tour.

Whether the cover picture and lead story on Hogan originated the so-called cover-story jinx associated with *Time* is debatable. It certainly contributed to the myth that being pictured on the cover of the magazine brought bad luck.

Twenty-three days after the cover story's publication Hogan was fighting for his life in an El Paso hospital.

9

There is strong suspicion in this quarter that this was the most remarkable feat in the entire history of sports./Red Smith, 1950

Hogan was not without trepidations as he prepared for his comeback attempt in the 1950 Los Angeles Open.

Would his legs be able to carry him through four rounds of tournament golf? And, depending on how much they bothered him, could he play well?

To people who suggested his effort might be premature,

he answered only, "I like that course." Hogan had won two L.A. Opens and the 1948 U.S. Open at Riviera.

"It's a possibility I'll play," he said as he boarded the train in Fort Worth. "But right now I can't say. I honestly don't know myself. I'll just have to wait and see how I'm feeling and how my game is working. One thing I can tell you for sure: I'm not going out there and shoot in the eighties."

On Friday, December 30, he played his first practice round at Riviera. It was only the fourth round since his accident nearly eleven months past. He shot a 69, two under par. On Saturday, though, he said his play was "pretty stinking. My putting was terrible."

How were his legs after two successive practice rounds? "Not bad," he said. Hogan wrapped his legs in elastic bandages from ankles to thighs to facilitate circulation. If the swelling in his legs became too painful, at night he sat in a bathtub of hot water liberally sprinkled with Epsom salts to ease the swelling.

Hogan, an ardent football fan, passed up the Rose Bowl on Monday and made his fourth practice tour of Riviera while Ohio State was beating California, 17–14, over in Pasadena. After his fifth foray on the course on Tuesday, on which Hogan shot a 72 with nines of 39-33, he announced he definitely would compete in the tournament. He seemed to have gained confidence, although the weather was colder than his liking.

One young professional entrant was sitting in the locker room complaining about the weather. "C'mon," said Hogan, heading for the course, "you'll never get any better sitting there."

In his final practice round on Wednesday, Hogan scored a 67 and said, "I feel better every day." He skipped play on Thursday to concentrate on hitting shots in the practice area.

The appearance of Hogan attracted golf writers and sports columnists from across the country. Herb Graffis, editor of *Golfing* and *Golfdom*, was there to confirm that the miracle he had wished for in the hospital at El Paso had actually occurred.

Chuck Curtis, the L.A. *Times* golf writer, may not have

believed in miracles but he believed in Hogan. Curtis picked Ben, Jimmy Demaret, and Sam Snead to battle it out for the title.

Whatever Hogan's efforts in the tournament produced, the dramatic possibilities were inherent. Already, in Hollywood, there were those who had seized on the idea of a feature movie about Hogan. And they could go out to Riviera and see some important ingredients being supplied for the script as they happened.

A record first-day throng of nine thousand gathered at Riviera, and they flocked to Hogan's gallery. Eric Monti and Johnny Bulla had reason to wonder if the pairings committee for the sponsoring L.A. Junior Chamber of Commerce disliked them. They were to play with Hogan the first two rounds, and it was not the most enviable of situations. The crowd stampeded for vantage points to see Hogan. Bulla and Monti wondered later if anyone saw a shot they made.

Under a warm midday sun, Hogan prepared to drive off the first tee. A movie camera whirred. Hogan stepped back from his ball and frowned.

Hogan asked that no photographs be taken, and a caddy appeared carrying a sign which read, "No Cameras, Please. Player's Request."

The outcry among news photographers, sports editors of the Los Angeles newspapers, the wire service representatives, and others was predictable. The Jaycee officials were forced to retreat. They ordered the sign removed after the eighth hole. But fans booed newspaper photographers.

After the round, a meeting was held and the ban was no longer in effect. Hogan was understandably desirous of avoiding any pictorial record of embarrassment he might suffer on the course. What if a leg gave out and he fell? Or the cameras zeroed in on him in a bad golfing predicament? But these were the risks he accepted when he teed off.

Much as they admired Hogan, a number of the other professionals were openly critical of the attempted photographic ban. Some thought it was inspired by those with a movie in mind, that if no photographs were made of Hogan in the tournament, the story would be fresher when it was put on film and released.

The Riviera regulars among the spectators did not see the Hogan who had thrilled them in 1947 and 1948 appearances on the course, nor did they expect to. Ben was erratic on the greens, and weariness on the back nine caused him to lapse into the old hook off the tee. But his 34-39—73 first round score was much lower than had been anticipated on Hogan's first competitive outing in eleven months. Golfers and gallery were elated. They noted he rested between shots on a red folding golf seat, that he limped more as the round progressed. But who could tell—he might get back to title contention in the coming months if this was any indication.

He said he would continue to play golf so long as he could drag a leg out on the course. And here he was doing just that, and playing pretty well, too. The 73 tied Hogan for sixteenth in the field. Ed Furgol led with a 68.

Hogan's game was more consistent, and his score reflected it in Saturday's second round. At the fifth hole, as Ben was addressing a two-foot putt for a par, sportscaster Bill Stern, riding in a jeep, crested the brow of a nearby hill.

"I am speaking softly now as . . ."

His voice carried to Hogan, who stopped, looked up, grinned, and stepped back. Stern kept quiet and Hogan sank the putt.

Hogan birdied the ninth hole to turn with a 34 again. He three-putted the eleventh, but then dropped a monstrous sixty-footer at the fourteenth for a birdie and holed a five-footer at the seventeenth for another. He came back in 35 for a 69, and everyone was looking at each other in stunned disbelief.

Not only was 90 percent of the gallery trodding after Ben, by now so were most of the other contestants. Once they finished their round, they headed back out to watch the man at work.

Toney Penna was among them. He noticed the tenseness of the fans as Ben lined up every shot, and he overheard the numerous remarks marveling at Hogan's recovery from the accident.

The surprising Hogan was tied for third with Ellsworth Vines with thirty-six-hole totals of 142, even par. Jerry Barber was in the lead with 69-68—137—and Henry Ransom was next with 72-67—139.

Rain washed out Sunday's scheduled third round. It may have been a blessing for Hogan. He was feeling the strain and was out in 39 and on the eleventh hole when play was stopped.

Hogan felt better on Monday. A thirty-foot putt at the third nipped into the cup for a birdie. He belted a seven-iron approach within three feet at the seventh for another birdie. His drive on the eighth hole hit a spectator but dropped safely, and his twelve-foot putt found the range for a three-under-par 32 on the front side.

Ben came back one over with a 37 with a bogey at ten, a birdie at eleven, a bogey at fourteen, and a bogey at fifteen before finishing with a seven-foot putt for a birdie at eighteen. If people had been disbelieving after the second round, they were ecstatic after this second straight 69. Hogan was in second place at 211 and only two strokes back of Barber, who had shot a 72 for 209. Ransom, in the threesome with Hogan, took a 75 for 214, the same total as Snead, who had plugged away with rounds of 71-72-71.

"I'm plenty tired," Hogan said after the fifty-four holes. But he tapped that reservoir of inner strength which he seemed to possess. The next day he achieved his third straight 69. He two-putted for a birdie on the first hole and sank a twelve-footer on the eighth for a 33. On the final nine he took a bogey six at the eleventh hole after two badly played wood shots, then at the fifteenth saw a putt estimated at eighty to ninety feet curl and disappear over the edge of the cup for a birdie and a 36.

His 280 total appeared to be a likely winner. Only one man on the course had a chance, and that was Snead, who was three under par after the fourteenth hole. He needed to birdie two of the remaining four holes just to tie Hogan.

He got neither of them at the fifteenth and sixteenth holes. When they stood on the tee at the seventeenth, Snead turned to Jack Burke, Jr., and said, "Looks like we need a couple of birdies, little friend." Sam got them. He holed a fourteen-foot putt at the seventeenth. As he studied the fifteen-foot putt on the eighteenth green, the multitudes were "oohing" and "aahhing" in the drama of the situation.

Near the green a young man sitting in a tree fell out when a limb broke. He crashed into some vines and bushes. People ran to look; and in the din Snead backed away from his putt. Then the man stuck up his head and yelled, "Don't worry, I'm all right!"

Snead sank the putt. In the uproar that followed, an estimated fifty fans lost their footing and came tumbling down the hill onto the green. One who fell was Leo Carrillo, the actor. He climbed out from under a lady who had fallen on top of him, helped her to her feet, and the two of them did an impromptu dance around the green.

Hogan's response was dour. "I wish he'd won it out there," said Ben. A play-off was the last thing his legs needed to undergo. And the play-off was postponed for a week until after the Bing Crosby event because rain again made Riviera unplayable.

Already, though, Hogan's comeback was complete, play-off or not. Graffis had wished for a miracle, but he did not expect one so magnificent. When Red Smith, the New York *Herald-Tribune* columnist whose sports-page prose was considered without peer in America, suspected it was the most remarkable feat in the entire history of sports, many agreed.

Very few were the people who did not monitor Hogan's progress in the Los Angeles Open. And most spent the week afterward wondering if he could ice the incredible sequence with a victory in the play-off.

Hogan and Snead returned to Riviera for their play-off on January 18, 1950. On that same day in Austin, Texas, the Texas Court of Criminal Appeals reversed the guilty verdict against bus driver Alvin Logan on the basis that the jury had not been selected according to state statute. The ruling was issued on February 3, a year and a day after the accident. Scant notice was paid to the decision.

Considerable attention was paid to Hogan and Snead, but their golf did not reciprocate. Snead did not play exceedingly well, and Hogan was worse. Snead scored a 72 and Hogan a 76 over the par 71 Riviera course.

Snead won $2,600 first-prize money and Hogan $1,900 for second. They split 50 percent of the gate receipts, each netting about $1,000 from the paid crowd of 2,901, which was swelled to twice that size by those who had gained free entry. A friend commiserated with Hogan: "Plenty unlucky today, Ben."

"Unlucky, hell!" Ben retorted. "That was just damned bad golf."

The play-off result did little to diminish the admiration for his comeback, however. Hogan still had some recuperating and building of strength before regaining his stamina and the ability to make consistently the shots that had been almost as much a trademark as his white billed caps.

But he was back. He would need some time to become stronger and sharper, and he would find it necessary to finesse the ball more to compensate for his physical impairment. He would become such a master at "management" that he began to say that the game was 80 percent management and 20 percent golf.

At the Masters that spring, the hills of that onetime Georgia nursery at Augusta took more of a toll on his legs than the usual golf course. He tied for fourth at 288, while Demaret won his third Masters with a 283.

In early May Hogan played the Greenbrier Invitational at White Sulphur Springs, West Virginia. The par 70 Old White course measured 6,368 yards, and Hogan whipped around it in 64-64-65-66 for a 259, which tied Nelson's record for seventy-two holes set in 1945. Hogan's total also beat Snead by ten strokes. But he did not attach much significance to the performance.

"I thought I played better at the Masters," said Ben. And the Old White victory did not signify that he was ready for the U.S. Open over a course such as Merion in Pennsylvania. That was the crown he wanted. He figured to find out at Colonial how close he was to the capability necessary for a serious bid in the Open.

Hogan's home course of Colonial was a very tough par 70 of 7,005 yards' length.

"It is the only course I ever played where a straight ball won't work," Hogan told Jim Trinkle of the *Star-Telegram*. "On one hole you gotta fade, on another you hook, and some you got to do both.

"Ordinarily, you can manufacture a game for a course with a hook or a fade and use it that week. This is the only course I've seen where you have to do both."

Colonial, which was host to the U.S. Open in 1941, had many of the characteristics the contestants faced on the Open course each year. It was unforgiving of a miss. An inch or two difference in where a miss occurred could mean the difference in a relatively good score or a high score.

Colonial is a much flatter course than the Augusta National. Even so, Hogan's performance indicated his game was sounder than it had been at the Masters. He walked at a slow pace and still limped, but once he was over the ball he was the picture of concentration again, and executing his shots with confidence and precision.

Hogan was more consistent at Colonial with rounds of 71-73-68-70 for 282, a very commendable total for the course. He tied E. J. (Dutch) Harrison for third behind Sam Snead, who won with 277, and Skip Alexander at 280.

Yet most of those unswayed by sentiment did not rank him highly as a threat in the Open at the Merion Cricket Club, Haverford, Pennsylvania. The brilliance of preaccident performances was beginning to show again, admittedly, but the foremost question was whether he could walk thirty-six holes in one day. The Open of that era required the third and fourth rounds to be played on Saturday. Hogan had not even tried to walk that far in a single day, and most shared the opinion the grind would be too much for him.

In Hollywood, 20th-Century-Fox was proceeding with the

preproduction preparations for the movie of Hogan's life, *Follow the Sun*. MCA Artists Limited had negotiated for Hogan and sold the rights for a movie on him for $50,000, of which the agency received 10 percent. Frederick Hazlitt Brennan was doing the screenplay. Glenn Ford was to play the role of Hogan and Anne Baxter the part of Valerie. Hogan was signed as technical adviser.

At Merion Hogan, playing carefully, maneuvered for a 72 and a 69 in the first rounds. This placed him two strokes back of Harrison, who also seemed to have benefited from the Colonial exposure.

Saturday was hectic as always through the early going of the Open's third round as contestants charged for the lead or fell back, shot themselves into or out of contention.

As the afternoon wore on, it became evident that none of the leaders was going to sweep out and settle the issue early. It also became clear that Hogan's legs were going to sustain him for the distance regardless of his weariness or what he finally shot.

George Fazio unobtrusively came into the clubhouse at 287, adding a closing 70 to his morning's 72. He drew little notice at the time, but the 287 looked better when Mangrum could only equal it with a 76. Hogan was making his way up the twelfth fairway only one over par for the fourth round when everyone realized, seemingly at once, that his steady progress combined with the high scores had put him into position to win.

If he could play the last seven holes in two over par, he would win his second Open championship in as many tries.

Hogan immediately dropped one of those shots to par. His approach at the twelfth bounded over the green, he chipped back, but missed his five-foot par putt. After parring the thirteenth and fourteenth, he needed only a thirty-inch putt for his par on the fifteenth. He missed it. At the 445-yard sixteenth, Hogan played very well for his par four. Then he failed to get his par three at the seventeenth.

His tee shot found a trap to the left of the upper deck of the terraced green about 230 yards out. He pitched neatly to within five feet but missed the putt. It was his third bogey in six holes, and winning was no longer the possibility. He had to par the eighteenth to tie Fazio and Mangrum.

The eighteenth was a long hole, a 458-yard par-four, which required two outstanding shots to reach the plateaued green. The second shot usually called for a fairway wood or a long iron. The gallery lined the fairway and ringed the green. Hogan hit a stout drive to good position in the fairway. He selected a two-iron and made what has become one of the classic shots in golf legend. Hogan put all of his prowess and years of experience and learning into the shot. The ball left the club head in a low trajectory and seemed to have started a bit toward the left side of the green. But so fast did Hogan's long irons propel the ball, hardly had it become airborne than the cheers started and the thousands broke for vantage points around the green.

There was no way for Hogan to know exactly where the ball had landed or come to rest. But he knew from his manner of hitting it and the reaction of the people that the ball must be somewhere very close to where he wanted it. The ball lay about forty feet to the left of the cup with the surface flat between the ball and the cup, which was cut to the back-right on the green. Hogan rolled the approach putt a yard past the hole, then firmly tapped the ball into the cup for his par and a tie for first.

"If there was ever an obvious spot for Hogan to blow a tournament," Demaret wrote, "it was there on the eighteenth. His lead had evaporated entirely. But this is the kind of spot in which Ben's iron discipline asserts itself. He walked up to the tee for the last hole of the tournament in perfect control. He slammed a long drive and then a whistling iron shot to a good spot on the green. He knocked in his second putt, a tough one to make, for a par and a tie."

Ben's routine of soaking in a hot tub appeared to have done wonders for him Saturday night. He seemed unusually fresh, considering that he had played four rounds in three days, when the play-off started on Sunday.

He was clearly superior in making his comeback complete. He shot a 69 to beat Mangrum by four strokes and Fazio by six. The issue was still in some doubt when they reached the sixteenth hole. Ben led Mangrum by one shot and Fazio by three. Hogan hit two magnificent shots and was eight feet from the cup. Mangrum had missed his drive but made it to the green in three after a fine pitch shot and was twelve feet from the hole. As Fazio lined up his putt, he asked Mangrum to mark his ball, since it was in his putting line.

After Fazio putted, Mangrum replaced his ball. Then, when Mangrum stepped up to putt, he noticed a bug on the ball. He picked up the ball and blew off the bug. Since USGA rules did not permit cleaning of the ball, Mangrum's act was an automatic two-stroke penalty. He sank the twelve-foot putt, Hogan missed his eight-footer, but Hogan had a four and Mangrum a six on the hole.

This was an unfortunate incident because to that point Mangrum was still very much in the hunt. Hogan removed some of the sting on the seventeenth hole, however, by banging a fifty-foot putt through a steep dip and into the cup for a birdie two. He thereby removed the penalty strokes as a major factor and ensured acceptance of his triumph for its clean-cut character.

Hogan parred the eighteenth hole for his four-stroke margin. He was back on top again.

Mangrum coolly commented, "Fair enough. We'll all eat tomorrow, no matter what happens."

A very tired Hogan said, "It's a great feeling. I thought the old legs would let me down some time or other and one of them did because I wrenched it. But I guess I'm pretty sound in wind and limb after all."

Snead won eight tournaments and Mangrum won five in 1950, but neither captured a major title. Ferrier won four events. Demaret won three, including the Masters. Chandler Harper won the PGA. The opposition was scattered. Hogan had won the U.S. Open and the Greenbrier, and tied for the L.A. Open in his first start after his accident. The spectacularly successful comeback weighed heavily in the voting and Hogan was named PGA Player of the Year.

The filming of his life story occupied much of Hogan's

remaining time that year. In helping Glenn Ford prepare for the starring role he was every bit the perfectionist and hard worker he was in golf.

The studio built a cage on the back lot with a target at the end. Ford hit ball after ball, and if he suggested taking a break, Hogan would say, "No, Glenn, I never let up."

The maddest Ford ever saw Ben was when they were sitting in a bar and a man from the studio brought in some of the poster display advertising sheets for the movie.

"This one said the movie was the story of two rollicking kids from Texas," Ford chuckled. "Hogan said could you imagine anyone describing him and Valerie as two rollicking kids, why he'd be laughed off the courses around the country. I told him, Ben, I'm with you on this."

Hogan made the golf shots in the movie, and a rubber mask was devised so he would look like Ford from the eyes down.

The world premier of *Follow the Sun* was held in Fort Worth in March 1951. Jimmy Demaret, Cary Middlecoff, and Sam Snead played themselves in the picture.

Hogan was defending his championship in the Greenbrier Invitation later that spring, and White Sulphur Springs and West Virginia were Snead's home grounds. Hogan said *Follow the Sun* was playing at one of the theaters there.

The theater marquee announced: "FOLLOW THE SUN, STARRING SAM SNEAD."

10

When Ben came back to our hotel room I made him a bet he'd be back in the Open next year. What would the Open be without my husband?/Valerie Hogan, 1955

Historically, the years 1948–55 came to be called "The Age of Hogan" in golf. His domination of the U. S. Open was the major reason.

     The formal name of the tournament is the United States Golf Association Open. But more commonly it was referred to as the U. S. Open, the National Open, or just the Open. Not since Bobby Jones in the 1923–30 era had a golfer been so close to invincible as Hogan in a major championship over so long a period of time.

Jones, an amateur, won his first Open in 1923 in a play-off with Bobby Cruickshank. In 1930 he won his fourth Open, his fifth U. S. Amateur, his third British Open, and his first British Amateur to score the unparalleled "Grand Slam."

Willie Anderson at the start of this century won four U. S. Opens in five years, three in succession. His scores, listed only for an interesting comparison to modern golf, were 331, 307, 303, and 314.

Hogan in 1951 was seeking his third straight Open—he was still recuperating from the accident and had been unable to compete in 1949.

Hogan was restricting his tournament golf to major events almost exclusively. He played the Colonial National Invitational in Fort Worth, as usual, in a final competitive tune-up for the Open, tying for fourth with two other contemporary war-horses, Byron Nelson and Ed (Porky) Oliver.

But as exacting as the Colonial course was, it could not prepare anyone for the Open scene of combat, Oakland Hills in the Detroit suburb of Birmingham. The tournament committee had called in golf architect Robert Trent Jones to revitalize the course and restore par to a meaningful figure. The membership generally was proud to point out that the only player who had broken 300 in the 1924 Open there was Cyril Walker.

Jones lengthened seven holes, added forty bunkers, and filled in the old traps flanking the fairways 200 to 220 yards from the tee, replacing them with ones of 220–235 yards out. More premium was placed on accuracy from the tee by narrowing the fairways, particularly those sections where most of the pros' average drives would land.

Jones and the tournament committee gained the instant unpopularity of every contestant arriving and seeing the course for the first time. Their descriptions of the 6,927-yard course were sprinkled with expletives.

Hogan was inclined to practice a little one-upmanship off the course when the opportunity arose. He preferred the major championships to be played on championship-caliber tracks. The truer the test of golf, the more likely the better golfer over the distance would win. And on such courses, Hogan was proving to be better a great percentage of the time.

At the Masters one year it appeared that the tournament committee would permit the Augusta National to play somewhat easier than normal, by pin placements and mowing of the greens.

Hogan predicted that the tournament record would be beaten that week. The committee was thus prompted to let the rough grow, tighten the pin placements, and generally toughen up the course until, when they teed off, Hogan said he would take a score of 290.

He used the same tactics at Baltusrol and Denver's Cherry Hills on other occasions. But for Oakland Hills, even Hogan could offer no suggestions to make the course tougher. He termed the place "ridiculous," and switched his one-upmanship to his old rival, Snead.

Hogan, citing the type of course it was and Snead's long-hitting ability off the tee and with the long irons, said it was the ideal site for Snead's chances to win his first Open.

Snead's response was to utter a naughty word and add with a big grin, "I know what that little man is doing."

Hogan by this stage in his career had proved he had some quality most others did not possess when it came to championship courses. On the tournament circuit as it moved around the United States, other golfers might seem to play as well and score comparably well. They hit the ball as far, scrambled out of trouble superbly, and putted phenomenally. Perhaps those were primarily the result of mechanical prowess.

When it came to the severe tests, Hogan's combination of determination, concentration, intelligence, courage, and management capabilities set him apart. Where in 1950 at Merion he had overcome inestimable odds to beat his rivals and bury the predictions of the medical profession, Hogan now was the man to beat. But few of the entries could worry about beating a man when they had such grave doubts about beating the course.

The Oakland Hills par of 280 for seventy-two holes was considered completely unattainable. The par of 70 for eighteen holes might be assailable, but few thought it would be attainable either. This was a course that offered Hogan's wits the most baffling battle yet. He was not quite sure through his practice rounds just how the course should be attacked. The place puzzled him. He was feeling good, thought his swing was right, even as he protested that the rough was too high.

Hogan reverted to use of his old center-shafted blade putter. He bent the blade "open" a little more than it had been. But the putter could not salvage the first round for him. He was on the wrong side of fairways and greens, over the putting surface with a couple of approaches, and over par by six strokes when he finished, the fury within him tightly restrained.

Not often did Hogan find himself tied for forty-first place at any stage of a tournament, although it placed him only five strokes back of the leader, Snead, who opened with a 71. That evening as he sat soaking his legs in the bathtub, Hogan diverted his dissatisfaction back to the strong positive attitude he always tried to maintain.

His negotiation of the course on the second round was considerably better, more so for the planning and execution than the mechanical aspects of scoring. He was not pleased with his 73. True, he had moved up to a tie for ninth, but he was still five strokes back of the leader, who after thirty-six holes was Bobby Locke at 144. Snead had tripped to a 78 and was bracketed with Hogan and Mangrum at the 149 figure. There were fifteen golfers ahead of Hogan.

That evening as he reviewed his position, Ben was not optimistic. "I'd have to be Houdini to win now," he said. "It would take 140 to get the lead and how can anyone shoot 140 on this course?"

The writers listening to him nodded in agreement. In their dispatches they wrote him off his Open throne as gracefully as possible. By the time their printed words hit the front steps the next morning, however, Hogan had run his cumulative knowledge of Oakland Hills through his computer brain and determined how the course should be played. Golf's growing popularity and the magnetism of Hogan lured an estimated fifteen thousand people to Oakland Hills for Saturday's final thirty-six holes. USGA executive director Joe Dey called it "the largest gallery in American golf history."

No player had gotten the best of par in either of the first two rounds, and only two had matched 70. Hogan began Saturday morning as if he were Houdini, after all. He birdied the first, second, and fifth holes and was three under par. This was the finest start anyone had made on a tournament round, and the spectators were exuberant with appreciation.

Ben drove into the creek at the seventh and lost one of the strokes to par. But he rammed in a thirty-five-foot birdie putt at the eighth to get it right back. He was three under with a 32 making the turn. The word spread, and people flocked to follow the back nine and see this David whip the Goliath of a course. Hogan got his pars through the thirteenth hole. But the giant, though staggered, had some resistance in reserve.

Hogan hit his long second over the green at the fourteenth, chipped back somewhat feebly, and two-putted for bogey. His drive at the fifteenth sent the ball rolling to a bad-lie stop in the rough. Hitting out with an iron, he sailed the ball across the fairway into the opposite rough.

His third shot was too weakly hit, and the ball fell into a bunker fronting the green. He blasted out and two-putted for a double-bogey six. He stood with his hands on his hips, his lips tightening and his eyes getting that look which prompted fellow pros to call them "steelies." He had lost the three strokes. He was even par.

Hogan's response was what it usually was when adversity struck—he struck back. He hit a perfect drive on the sixteenth tee to lay the ball up next to the edge of the lake. The cup was set over to the right of the green, which nosed well out into the water, and the pin was a high-risk target.

Hogan's overnight calculations convinced him that this was no day for prudence, and the six at fifteen was in his craw.

He drilled his approach shot directly at the pin, and the ball stopped five feet away. He did not make the birdie putt, but he had played the hole as beautifully as it could be played, betraying no loss of confidence in his sound swing and showing he was not conceding anything.

Ben dropped another stroke to par when he failed on a four-foot putt at the seventeenth. His 71 was his best effort, and an excellent score, but it was disappointing, too. He had the giant down and let it get up.

Still, first place was nearer. Locke had taken a 74 for 218, and Jimmy Demaret's 70 tied the South African for the lead. Julius Boros and little Paul Runyan were at 219. Hogan and Clayton Heafner stood at 220. A quick lunch of roast beef did not lighten the mood remaining with Hogan from the morning's finish. He set out grimly, and told Dey, who was refereeing, "I'm going to burn it up this afternoon."

But the front nine did not yield as it had before the break. Hogan put his two-iron tee shot over the green into a trap at the 200-yard third hole and took a bogey four. He regained that at the seventh with a brassie tee shot, a seven-iron approach and a two-foot putt. He was level at 35 with nine holes of the Open left to play.

Locke was just beginning his final round, and others among the leaders were scattered about the premises. There would be no man-to-man strategy—it was Hogan against the course, and his plotting of what he needed on the final nine represented a formidable assignment. He clearly revealed his intentions on the tenth hole. Some thought the 448-yard tenth the hardest par four on the course.

Hogan screamed his drive 260 yards down the fairway. He selected a two-iron for his second and rifled it to within four feet of the pin.

"My best shot of the tournament," he said later. "It went exactly as I played it every inch of the way."

Hogan tapped in the putt for a birdie three, then parred the eleventh and twelfth. He holed a fourteen-foot putt for a birdie on the thirteenth. But a three-iron second shot over the green cost

Valerie Hogan in April 1935—photo was printed with news of wedding to Ben Hogan in *Fort Worth Star-Telegram*. *(Fort Worth Star-Telegram Photo)*

Ben Hogan figures his assets in August 1937. *(Fort Worth Star-Telegram Photo)*

Hogan in follow through watches flight of the ball in Colonial National Invitational action of the 1940s. *(Photo by Al Panzera)*

Ben and Valerie Hogan in train compartment en route from El Paso to Fort Worth April 1, 1949, after release from hospital. *(Photo by Al Panzera)*

Hogan blasts from a difficult lie in a trap onto the fourth green in the first round of the 1953 Masters. *(Wide World Photos)*

Hogan lines up putt which he sank on eighteenth green for record 72-hole score of 274 in 1953 Masters Tournament. Cardboard periscopes were a big thing with galleries in those years. *(Wide World Photos)*

Hogan lifts his ball from a trap on the eighth hole as he starts down the home stretch in the 1953 Open. *(Wide World Photos)*

Hogan drives from the third tee in the first round of the 1953 Open. *(Wide World Photos)*

Hogan in 1953 after winning the U.S. Open Golf Championship for the fourth time, becoming the third man to perform the feat. *(Wide World Photos)*

Hogan tries a chip shot during the first round of the 1953 British Open. *(Wide World Photos)*

Hogan after winning the 1953 British Open to complete golfdom's "triple crown." *(Wide World Photos)*

Exchange Alley in Manhattan's Wall Street district momentarily
becomes Ben Hogan's Alley as he moves up lower Broadway on
his return from winning the 1953 British Open.
(Wide World Photos)

Ben and Valerie Hogan and
Glenn Ford at March 1951 world
premiere of *Follow the Sun,*
movie based on Hogan's
comeback. *(Photo by
Al Panzera)*

Ben and mother, Clara Hogan, at Fort Worth
airport reception upon his return from British
Open victory in 1953. *(Photo by Al Panzera)*

"The Hawk" watches ball after shot during one of his infrequent appearances in the 1960s. *(Fort Worth Star-Telegram Photo)*

him a stroke at the fourteenth. He was one under for the round and now faced the fifteenth, where he had taken the six that morning. As he demonstrated so often in his career, he had learned his lesson well. He carried the bunker in the middle of the fairway with a four-wood from the tee, lofted a six-iron approach four feet from the pin and sank the putt. He had taken half the strokes required that morning and was two under par.

On the 405-yard "lake hole," the sixteenth, Hogan unwound on his drive to fly the ball 290 yards. From the side of the lake he snapped a nine-iron approach four feet from the cup but missed the putt. He parred the 194-yard seventeenth. Still two under. And now reports from around the course were beginning to filter to him. Among the earlier starters, Demaret had faded, Boros was struggling, and Heafner was maintaining a pace close to Ben's own. Locke was having trouble on the front nine.

Hogan thought a par four at the eighteenth, which measured 459 yards and was a heavily bunkered dogleg to the right, might bring him home the winner by a stroke. There was a slight wind to his back, and Hogan decided to try to sail his tee shot over the bunkered ridge in the angle of the dogleg. He unleashed another cannon shot of 280 yards from the tee and carried the ridge, leaving only a six-iron second to the green.

He hit it high and the ball floated down to the middle of the green, bit and stopped about fifteen feet from the pin. Rather than "lag" the ball for a cinch par and a 68, which might have won, Hogan gave the putt a chance to drop. He rolled the ball gently to the cup, and it plopped out of sight for a birdie three.

Hogan had shot 35-32—67—three under par over a course that was probably the sternest challenge ever offered a U.S. Open field. It was the lowest eighteen-hole score of the tournament and only one of two below 70 in the entire event. Heafner came in behind Ben with the other, a 69.

Hogan's "Houdini" act on Saturday netted him a round-by-round improvement of 76-73-71-67, a score of 138 on the closing thirty-six holes, for a seventy-two-hole count of 287. Par of 280 had withstood the field. Heafner was second with 289.

"Under the circumstances," said Hogan, "it was the

greatest round I have played. I didn't think I could do it. My friends said last night that I might win with a pair of 69s. It seemed too much on this course. It is the hardest course I ever played. I haven't played all the courses in the world, but I don't want to, especially if there are any that are tougher than this one.''

Ben's attitude toward the course wasn't mollified by the satisfaction of winning his third Open in as many tries, or by a final-round performance that would stand as the best, at least one of the three best, of his career.

"I'm glad,'' he said at the presentation ceremonies, "that I brought this course, this monster, to its knees.''

Hogan raised his fee for exhibitions to $1,000, and played fifteen the remainder of the year. There were squawks from many club professionals, who usually arranged such affairs to spur interest among members, that Ben was being greedy, not giving back to golf what he had gotten out of it. Hogan knew what he was doing. Golf was his business, too, and if he could lead the way to more lucrative levels and attract more young men to the profession, golf would thrive beyond anyone's imagination.

The other ''name'' players were not shy about following his precedent. After winning the PGA that year, Snead raised his exhibition fee to $800. "If Hogan's worth a thousand,'' drawled Sam, "I oughta be worth eight hundred.''

Ben played on the 1951 Ryder Cup team which defeated the British, 9½–2½, on the Pinehurst No. 2 course in North Carolina. Henry Longhurst, the British journalist—and a golfer of some skill, too—accompanied the invaders for the matches and other competition in the States.

"I watched Hogan closely in a practice round with Jackie Burke, Demaret and Claude Harmon,'' wrote Longhurst in some recollections of the trip:

Each of those three was driving a colossal sort of ball which, when it should have been descending, would bore onwards towards the hole, and it seemed impossible that a man the size of Hogan, who happened to be driving last, could reach them.

Time and again, however, he lashed the ball along thirty

feet from the ground, or "quail high" as they say in Texas. It ran perhaps thirty yards to where theirs had stopped almost dead on the soft fairways, and finished five yards best of the lot.

Since then I have been consulting his book, "Power Golf," to see whether, unlike so many golfers who write books, he practices what he preaches. The answer is, "Yes he does." I never saw anything quite like it. By taking his club far away from him on the backswing, and then almost as far back round his neck as our own James Adams, and then thrusting it even farther away in front after impact he attains, in fact, the swing of at least a six-footer.

His right arm never bends after impact and it finishes in a position with which the middle-aged reader may care at his own risk to experiment, namely dead straight and pointing, almost horizontally, behind his head. "The speed and momentum," says the caption, "have carried me to a full finish." They would carry most of us to the infirmary.

Hogan is a fascinating study, almost as fascinating, in an opposite way, as was Hagen, with whose name his own used so often to be confused. Hagen was colourful, eccentric, theatrical, gregarious. He loved wine and women and his fellowmen, from caddies to Prince of Wales, and saw no reason why life should not permanently be standing him a bottle of champagne.

Hogan is the reverse of the coin—steel-hard, wiry, self-disciplined, austere. Hagen was a gift to golf writers. Of Hogan, till his motor smash and subsequent recovery made him an idol of sporting America, they could find little to say except that he had again gone round in 68. . . . The answer to Hogan is, I fancy, that if Hogan means to win, you lose.

One day at Pinehurst Hogan was practicing, hitting towering wood shots, when Max Faulkner of the British team walked up and volunteered, "I say, Ben, I think I could help you with that fade. If you'd drop your right hand under the shaft a bit, you'd cure the fade."

Hogan looked at Faulkner stonily and replied, "You don't see the caddie moving any, do you?"

Hogan was named the PGA Golfer of the Year for the

third time, and in December 1951 was voted into the Texas Sports Hall of Fame, only the second person so honored. The first was Tris Speaker, famed "Grey Eagle" of baseball.

In 1953, Ben Hogan hit more pure golf shots than most players do in a lifetime. Many were originals and not many have been duplicated. He played such superb golf that it appeared he could win almost as many tournaments as he wanted, or was physically able, to enter. He was forty years old.

He wanted that fourth Open to draw abreast of Jones and Anderson and a fifth to break their record. The Open that year was to be held at Oakmont, Pennsylvania, a course with infamously-fast greens.

Oakmont's 6,916-yard par-72 course was a test, all right, but deemed somewhat easier than it was when the Open was held there in 1935 and Sam Parks was the only entry to break 300. Hogan defied the twenty-year-old halfway leader jinx by taking early command.

This time he led off with a ripping five-under-par 67, and the drama remaining consisted of Snead being the pursuer and Hogan's blistering finish. Hogan added a 72 for a thirty-six-hole lead of 141, three under par and two strokes ahead of Snead. For most of Saturday's two rounds the Open was a two-man duel. Then it became a one-man show.

Hogan faded slightly on the morning tour with a 73, and Snead closed within a shot with a 72. They both turned the front nine in the afternoon at 38. Half the fans watched Hogan to see if he could win his fourth Open. The other half followed Snead to see if he could win his first.

Snead said he had figured out how to play the course. "You gotta sneak up on these holes," he remarked. "If you clamber and clank up on 'em, they're liable to turn around and bite you."

Sam was bitten on the twelfth hole of the fourth round. He tried to charge with his second shot on the 598-yard stretch, mis-hit the fairway wood, and needed three to reach the green. There he three-putted for a bogey six.

Hogan made Snead's six inconsequential to the outcome.

At the sixteenth Ben struck a fine wood shot from the tee and dropped the ball onto the small green 234 yards away. He two-putted for a par three. At the strange seventeenth, which was 292 yards uphill and a par four, Hogan hit a shot reminiscent of his two-iron second to the final green at Merion in 1950. He cranked out his best pop of the tournament and flew the ball between the sentinel traps and onto the green. He two-putted for a birdie three.

At the eighteenth, a par four of 462 yards, Hogan pumped a drive of almost 300 yards, leaving him merely a medium five-iron approach to the green. This he struck, and the ball nestled down nine feet past the cup. He rolled the ball gently into the hole for a birdie three. The 3-3-3 spurt at the wire brought him in with a 38-33—71—for the closing round and a total of 283. It was the first time Oakmont par of 288 had submitted in competition over the seventy-two hole route.

Snead faded as the futility of his pursuit became evident. He carded a 76 and was second at 289. Hogan joined Anderson and Jones as the only four-time winners of the Open. But his sights were now firmly set on a fifth. More and more good young players were joining the tour, though, and the chances were diminishing with the passage of time. Hogan was getting a bit long in the tooth at forty-one years of age when the next opportunity arrived in 1954.

Hogan was named PGA Player of the Year for the fourth time in 1953. Until 1962, no other golfer ever won the honor more than once. And not until 1975 when Jack Nicklaus earned the honor for the fourth time was the record matched.

Hogan also was elected to the PGA Hall of Fame and voted Male Athlete of the Year in the United States in the Associated Press poll.

Two weeks before the 1955 Colonial Invitational, Hogan said, "I just can't seem to get up any enthusiasm." He played the event in a relaxed manner unlike his former self. And after finishing he said he was "through playing serious golf." With the Open coming up, Hogan had gone almost two years without a major championship.

He was definitely slowing down some, missing a fairway

more often and short putts even more often. Although still a consummate shotmaker, Hogan was rated by one handicapper as no better than 15-1 to win the Open. When he arrived at the Olympic Club in San Francisco, he said, "If I'm lucky enough to win here, I doubt if I will ever play in an important tournament again. It's just too hard." He was two months shy of his forty-third birthday.

His rivals, and most competent observers, had learned to ignore such pronouncements. They knew that when it came to a major championship "The Hawk" would be in the hunt.

Olympic's Lakeside course was the object of almost as many players' complaints as Detroit's Oakland Hills. The rough was a jungle, the fairways narrow, the greens small, and the traps tight. Par was 70. Hogan's plan was to play close to the vest, keep the ball shorter and in play, and avoid the matted rough which lined the fairways and hemmed in the aprons of the greens.

Tommy Bolt had played some rounds with Hogan in Fort Worth, and they had been a tonic to him. He came to San Francisco convinced he could win, and Bolt's three-under-par 67 in the first round had others sharing his belief. Bolt was five ahead of Hogan, who started with a 72, and nine strokes ahead of a thirty-two-year-old club professional from Davenport, Iowa, named Jack Fleck.

Fleck's best previous Open finish was a tie for fifty-second in 1953. Hardly anyone except Charlie Newman was paying attention to Fleck, and Newman had a reason. He was manager of the Ben Hogan Company, which manufactured golf clubs in Fort Worth. Fleck was playing with a set of Hogan clubs, and Newman had completed the set only the Monday before the Open by bringing several wedges to San Francisco for Fleck to try.

Snead, a pretournament favorite, was almost gone before he got started. He shot an opening 78 and but for his putter would have soared into the 80s. Bolt could not keep the touch. Hogan remained steady with a second-round 73. Fleck apparently was gaining confidence in his new clubs. His second-round 69 tied him with Hogan at 145.

Hogan nursed it around for a 72 Saturday morning; Fleck had a 75. While the few other contenders surrendered to the rough and other misfortunes, Hogan, manipulating the ball carefully, matched par of 70 in the closing round. He walked off the final green thinking he had won his fifth Open by five strokes.

"Here, Joe," said Hogan, handing the ball with which he had finished the tournament to USGA executive director Joe Dey, "this is for Golf House." Hogan referred to the USGA museum to which he had already contributed much.

Hogan was not alone in the belief he had won. Those surrounding him as he sat before his locker sipping a Scotch and water shared his high spirits. No one, apparently, could catch him. Oh, there was word that one player named Fleck still had a mathematical possibility. He was on the fourteenth fairway when a friend informed him that Hogan had finished with a score of 287.

"Now I know I have a chance," Fleck said. He may have been the only person in San Francisco to think so. After he took a bogey five at the 410-yard fourteenth hole, Fleck needed two birdies on the last four holes to tie. That was asking a great deal even of seasoned veterans.

Fleck did not blanch. He holed a ten-foot putt for a birdie deuce at the fifteenth, or sixty-ninth, hole. He parred the next two and narrowly missed birdie efforts on both. So he was at the last hole, the 337-yard eighteenth, still in quest of a birdie to tie.

Told of this in the locker room, Hogan set down his glass, said, "Good luck to him," and headed for the shower. Fleck's three-wood tee shot on the seventy-second hole bounced high off a slope and came to rest sitting prettily in the short rough three feet left of the fairway.

He selected a seven-iron for his second shot. He lofted the ball high over a bunker to the sharply sloping green, and it settled about ten feet from the cup. Fleck gave himself no time to become tense. From the time he studied the line of the putt until he took his stance and stroked the ball only twenty-four seconds elapsed. The ball rolled dead-center into the cup for a closing 67, which matched Hogan's 287.

Despite the dramatic conclusion to the play-off, putting was the difference. Fleck used twenty-nine putts and had seven one-putt greens in scoring a 69. Hogan required thirty-two putts, had five one-putt greens and one three-putt green, the twelfth, for a 72.

Fleck holed a twenty-five-foot birdie putt at the ninth and a seventeen-footer at the tenth for a three-stroke lead over Hogan in the play-off. Hogan got one of the shots back at the fourteenth and another at the seventeenth. But on the eighteenth tee it was Hogan carrying the burden of getting a birdie for a possible tie.

Hogan did not set himself firmly in the loam of the tee, and his right foot slipped as he drove the ball. It hooked sharply far off the fairway into the thick rough. On his first effort at getting the ball out, Hogan's club head carried almost a pitcherful of matted growth farther than the ball, which was four feet. It took him two more hacks to get the ball out onto the fairway. From there, naturally, he went for the pin. The ball sailed thirty-five feet past the cup on the uphill back side. He was lying five.

Fleck had his par all the way. Deprived of his fifth Open, Hogan now faced the distinct possibility of three-putting for an embarrassing eight before the multitudes around the green. Limping noticeably, his face grim and wan, physically exhausted, Hogan roused himself for a memorable moment. He barely tapped the ball on its fast downhill path. The ball rolled down the slope and slipped into the cup for a six.

Being tied and then losing the play-off was among the most gut-wrenching experiences of Hogan's life. Victory at San Francisco would have climaxed an amazing career of competitive golf and placed Hogan on a pedestal above all who had ever played the game.

Disappointed? The word was far from adequate in describing his emotions. "Yes, but you get used to that in this game," he said.

His pale features gradually changed from the grim look of a loser to a smile as he walked to Fleck and congratulated the winner. He took his cap and grinned as he fanned Fleck's putter to the delight of the photographers.

In the days following the tournament Hogan seemed wearier than he had in several years. And on his return to Fort Worth there were no brass bands or police escort to greet him. "The Age of Hogan" was considered at an end by the game's historians. It would be a few more years, however, before an answer was forthcoming to Valerie's question about what the Open would be without her husband.

Although he was within contending distance at times in the remaining years of the fifties, it was at Denver's Cherry Hills in 1960 that he made his last, valiant, and serious bid for that fifth Open championship.

Par at Cherry Hills was 35-36—71—and the course played about 400 yards shorter than its listed length of 7,004. Hogan started the tournament with a respectable score for a man nearing his forty-eighth birthday. He shot a 75. Mike Souchak led with a 68, and the burly former football player maintained the pace through both the second and third rounds with 67-73 for a 208 total.

Hogan swept back with scores of 67 and 69 for a 211, paired with twenty-year old U. S. Amateur champion Jack Nicklaus the last thirty-six holes. As they began the final round, eighteen players were ranged from Souchak's 208 to the 215 shared by Arnold Palmer and others.

After the lunch break, the scramble turned into a reenactment of the Oklahoma land rush. Souchak's bogey five at the sixty-third hole knocked him out of the lead for the first time in the tournament, and Nicklaus, on the sixty-sixth, took over. Palmer started with six birdies on the first seven holes.

Hogan was only two strokes back of Nicklaus when he played the sixty-fourth hole, the tenth of the final round. At one point at least twelve players still had an opportunity to win. Nicklaus, Boros, Jack Fleck, who was at 212 after fifty-four holes, and Palmer were tied for the lead.

Ben was on the green at the sixty-ninth, or fifteenth, hole, his ball about eight feet from the cup. Aileen Covington, editor of a West Coast golf magazine, told him if he made the putt he would be tied with the field. He made it. Hogan got his par on the seventieth hole, the sixteenth of the round. His calculator-like mind was as sharp as ever. He assembled the other players' progressive scores as they were fed to him. He digested the information, and at the seventy-first hole, the par-five seventeenth, the conclusion he reached was that a birdie and a par on the last two holes could win the tournament by a stroke.

"I didn't have a chance to birdie eighteen," he said later. "So I thought I had to birdie the seventeenth."

Hogan knew the course, knew the players, and knew the pressures of the Open. He went for the birdie on the seventy-first hole. He hit his drive well, then a four-iron put the ball short of the lagoon which almost surrounded the elevated green. He had learned from the morning's round not to hit his pitch shot beyond the hole—he needed the ball close but on the downward side of the cup.

"I tried to put as much stuff on the ball as I could to hold it this side of the hole," he said. He put so much "bite" on the ball that when it hit, it sucked back down the slope and came to rest almost covered by the water at the edge of the lagoon.

Hands on hips, half-smoked cigarette drooping from his tightly pursed lips, Hogan looked at the ball which could have meant so much to him. Then he sat down and started taking off his right shoe.

"The old boy's going for it!" the spectators cried. And there was a roar of approval. Hogan had never defaulted to a course before, and he was not about to do so at this critical juncture. He rolled up his right trousers leg, took a stance with his right foot planted in the lagoon, and splashed the ball out in a desperate attempt for a birdie four. The ball landed on the green, but not in the cup. He two-putted for a bogey six. He then took a triple-bogey seven on the seventy-second hole. He finished 6-7 for 284.

He had made his bid and lost. But that was the only way he knew. He never played for second. His assessment of what was required of him on the last two holes was accurate. He had figured a 4-4 finish would win the Open by a stroke, which would have given him a seventy-two-hole score of 279. Palmer's closing 65 won at Cherry Hills with 280.

Instead of a 68, Hogan shot a 73. Instead of winning his fifth Open, he tied for ninth in his seventeenth Open. "The Age of Hogan" actually ended at Cherry Hills' seventeenth hole in 1960.

That a man could have played so well so regularly for so long in the major championship of golf is almost beyond belief. Sarazen's longevity was remarkable and Jones's record in eight years was awesome. But neither before nor since has a golfer performed so consistently well over such a span of time as Hogan did in the U. S. Open from 1940 to 1960.

In the fifteen Opens he played in those two decades, Hogan averaged 286.3 strokes per seventy-two holes. The average winning score of those Opens was 283.1 strokes. His average score for sixty non-play-off, Open rounds was 71.58 strokes. His average score for 1,080 holes of Open competition was 3.97 strokes.

He had the most sub-par rounds of any player from 1940 to 1960 with eighteen. He had the most rounds of par or better for the period with twenty-five. He scored 72 or better in thirty-eight of the sixty rounds of Open competition. He shot the most rounds under 70 with fourteen. And he set the Open record of 276 at Los Angeles in 1948, broken by Nicklaus's 275 in 1967 at Baltusrol.

After the final-round 80 and total of 308 at Philadelphia in the 1939 Open, Hogan for the next two decades had no single round over 77 and only one seventy-two-hole score worse than 290—the 294 at Southern Hills in 1958.

He won four Opens, was second twice, and missed a title play-off by a stroke another time. He was always up there threatening—tenth place in fifteen Opens was his worst finish.

Two shots in two Opens years afterward were singled out by Hogan as his greatest disappointments in competitive golf. The first was the drive at 18 in the 1955 play-off with Fleck.

"When I walked up on the tee I could see that it had not been watered," said Hogan. "I should have worked my feet into the soil just like you do in a sand trap to anchor my right foot. But I didn't."

The resultant hook buried the ball in the rough to the left of the fairway. The other disappointment was the third shot on the seventeenth hole of the final round at Denver in 1960.

"I laid up to the lake with a four-iron and had the most beautiful lie you could have," he said. "The way I was putting, I knew I had to get within two feet or I couldn't possibly make it. I played what I thought was a good shot, but it hit on the edge of the green and then was drawn back into the water by the backspin. It was hit exactly as I intended, but I just misjudged the shot."

The surprise in this recap of Hogan's record in the U.S. Open is not that he won four times. The surprise is that he did not win five, six, or even seven Opens:

Ben Hogan's Record
THE UNITED STATES GOLF ASSOCIATION OPEN,
1940–60

Canterbury GC, Cleveland, Ohio
1940   70-73-69-74—290   Tied for fifth

Colonial CC, Fort Worth, Tex.
1941   74-77-68-70—289   Tied for third

1942–45   No tournaments played.

Canterbury GC, Cleveland, Ohio
1946   72-68-73-72—285   Tied for fourth

St. Louis CC, St. Louis, Mo.
1947   70-75-70-74—289   Tied for sixth

Riviera CC, Los Angeles
1948   67-72-68-69—276 (New record by five strokes.)   Winner

Medinah CC, Medinah, Ill.
1949   Did not play, injuries.

Merion GC, Ardmore, Pa.
1950   72-69-72-84—287   Winner (Tied for first, won play-off.)

Oakland Hills CC, Birmingham, Mich.
1951   76-73-71-67—287   Winner

Northwood CC, Dallas, Tex.
1952   69-69-74-74—286   Third

Oakmont CC, Oakmont, Pa.
1953   67-72-73-71—283   Winner

Baltusrol CC, Springfield, N.J.
1954   71-70-76-72—289   Tied for sixth

Olympic CC, San Francisco
1955   72-73-72-70—287   Second (Tied for first, lost play-off.)

Oak Hill CC, Rochester, N.Y.
1956   72-68-72-70—282   Tied for second

Inverness Club, Toledo, Ohio
1957   Did not play, illness.

Southern Hills CC, Tulsa, Okla.
1958   75-73-75-71—294   Tied for tenth

Winged Foot CC, Mamaroneck, N.Y.
1959   69-71-71-76—287   Tied for eighth

Cherry Hills CC, Denver, Colo.
1960   75-67-69-73—284   Tied for ninth

Number of U. S. Opens played:	15
Hogan's average score per Open:	286.3
Average winning score per Open:	283.1
Hogan's average score per round, 60 rounds:	71.58
Hogan's average score per hole, 1,080 holes:	3.97
Hogan's number of Open rounds, 72 or better:	38 (63%)

Figures do not include play-off rounds.

11

A great player finally rendered a very great service to the Masters Tournament by adding his name to its list of champions. Ben Hogan had played enough good golf on the Augusta National course to win, with a little luck, several first prizes. Each year that he failed the number of well-wishers grew until in 1951, one of the largest galleries ever to support an individual player brought Ben in the winner./Clifford Roberts, 1952

Through his first nine Masters Tournaments Ben Hogan possessed one of only two sub-par scoring averages, yet he had not won the event. His 71.97 strokes per round performance was second by Byron Nelson's 71.88 in thirteen appearances. And Nelson had won twice.

Hogan lost the 1942 title in a play-off with Nelson. And Ben three-putted the final green in 1946 to miss tying Herman Keiser for the championship. The Hogan timetable always seemed to be out of kilter with others' expectations. Everything kept happening later than it was anticipated. Demaret, his good friend, had won three Masters by 1950. Snead had won his first in 1949.

The Masters rated as one of the three major American golf classics, and was second only to the U. S. Open in prestige. The British Open and the PGA Championship joined those two as the quartet of premier achievements available to the tournament golfers of the world. Hogan no longer could play the match-play PGA affair because of its required thirty-six holes per day. But he had won two PGAs and the Open twice.

And everyone expected Hogan to complete the American triumvirate by winning the Masters. When that tournament's fifteenth edition neared in 1951, no doubts remained concerning his physical ability to play championship golf again. He had convinced his rivals with his U. S. Open victory at Merion.

Close observers believed Hogan was becoming an even surer, more confident shotmaker than before his accident. This was largely because of compensation for the reduced strength in his legs. He was plotting and planning his pace and play in relation to the course and competition in a thoroughness never before attempted by a golfer.

He had not lost one degree of determination and was as demanding of himself as ever in practice and tournament action. But he was now increasingly demanding of his mental rather than his physical powers, stressing the "management" phases of the game. His will to win was undiminished by success. Sarazen's word picture of Hogan as a "perpetually hungry" golfer was still true in every respect.

For men who loved golf with the passion of Ben Hogan, the Masters became something of a shrine to the game and the annual pilgrimage a special pleasure. Bobby Jones as a founder of the Augusta National Club and the tournament gave the place instant credibility and acclaim, and hastened recognition of the annual event as a classic.

Rare is the course that has been designed so well to offer both the player and the spectator enjoyment. Carved from a nurseryland through the pines and across rolling terrain of eastern Georgia, the course was aesthetically unexcelled, especially when the dogwood, azaleas, and camellias were in bloom to accent the various shades of green which met the eye after the mist of an April morning melted before the rising sun's rays.

The presence of Jones and other past masters of the game contributed much to the feeling that this was the ultimate in golfing environment, the Valhalla where old golfing warriors might go when they putted out for the last time.

Hogan's sentiments regarding Augusta National and the Masters were well known. The course was the setting for the photographs of his swing and other illustrations included in his instruction book, *Power Golf*. And as Clifford Roberts, chairman of the tournament committee since its inception, noted, sentiment for Hogan to win the Masters had grown through every year he failed.

By 1951, Ben's restricted schedule of competition started with the Masters. He might have played in some event such as the Thunderbird Invitational in Palm Springs or the Seminole Pro-Am in Palm Beach, but the Masters was where he became really serious.

The Augusta National course, measuring 6,900 yards and playing to par of 36-36—72, was deceptive. Most fairways were wide and inviting, and the greens were large. A duffer might actually score better there than on his home course. But it was a different track in the four days of the tournament. The large greens not only had undulations which some described as elephant graves but were mowed to a shortness and hardened to such a crispness that Hogan once said walking on them "sounded like you were walking on straw. They'd crackle. It was impossible to get down from thirty-five feet in two. The undulations made it where you had to be almost inside twelve feet to get down in two."

The pin placements on the greens were selected from a master chart each day after consideration of the wind and weather conditions. The chart gave four preferred positions for each green, and the cups rarely varied more than three feet from one of those spots from year to year. The greens committee tried to give the contestants six "easy," six medium-hard, and six difficult placements each round. But if the scores ran particularly low, the ratio of difficult pin placements usually rose the next day.

The wind blowing through the majestic pines created the soothing sounds of a reed-orchestra symphony for some. But it created some sick feelings among golfers through the years. On the holes where water added to the hazards, the eleventh, twelfth, and thirteenth notably, and the fifteenth and sixteenth, the winds could be terribly tricky. A golfer teeing off in the calm at the short par-three twelfth might see his ball soar as intended toward the pin, only to have it come into contact with the wind up at the treetops and suddenly plummet into the pond below.

Most of the heartbreak and much of the drama of the Masters occurred on that back nine. Demaret gained seven strokes on six holes when he won over Ferrier in 1950. In 1937 Nelson was chasing Guldahl. Guldahl scored a five at the twelfth and a six at the thirteenth, Nelson shot a two and a three, picked up six shots on the two holes, and won his first Masters.

Two days prior to the 1951 Masters two writers were walking and talking with Bobby Jones, whose progress from the clubhouse to his cottage was slow because of the brace on his right leg and the necessity to use a cane. One of the many Pinkerton men who formed security for the Masters interrupted to ask Jones what should be done about those baseball players from Boston who did not have tickets.

"Leave them alone," Jones answered. The Red Sox were in Augusta for a spring exhibition game, and several of the players had come out to meet and watch the professional golfers. Up in the clubhouse Fred Corcoran was introducing baseball players to golfers. Ted Williams was standing as he shook hands with a man sitting on the shoe locker bench. Williams turned to Corcoran and said, "I just shook a hand that felt like five bands of steel." Williams and Hogan had met.

Each had admired the other, understandably. The great Red Sox hitter applied to baseball the same thorough approach Hogan did to golf. Both studied their sport diligently and worked hard to improve. The two were similar in many ways.

There would be no high drama in the fifty-one Masters, although Skee Riegel gave it an element of spice by moving out front after thirty-six holes and remaining in contention to the finish.

Hogan, playing steady if unspectacularly, scored 70 and 72 and was a stroke back of Riegel at the halfway point. Snead with a 68 joined Riegel, with a 70, at 211 leading the field into the final eighteen holes. Hogan's 70 placed him a shot behind at 212.

As he sat pulling on his spiked shoes for the last round, a bystander idly remarked, "Guess you'd really like to win this one, eh, Ben, since you've never won a Masters."

"I try to win them all," Hogan replied. "But you're probably right. This one may mean something special."

"Looks like there'll be a tie and a play-off," commented the man.

"Don't think so," said Hogan, departing for the first tee. Hogan was the last of the leaders to take the course.

He issued his challenge quickly. A long, winding putt at the 535-yard second hole found the cup for a birdie four. He spanked his iron approach shot dead to the pin on the third for a birdie three. Hogan was going to the eighth tee when informed that Riegel had shot a 71 for 282, a score good enough to have won more than half the previous Masters.

Snead, hearing of Hogan's start, knew he needed to gamble some to remain in the chase. He struck two balls into the water guarding the left and rear of the eleventh green, took an eight on the hole, and was out of it, eventually scoring an 80 for the day.

"You're home free," fellow pros told Riegel up in the clubhouse. "I'd take that 282 and sit on it. Nobody'll beat that today."

"Wish you were right," Riegel responded. "I'd feel comfortable if it was anybody but that little guy out there."

Hogan's quick calculation at the eighth hole concluded that he had to play the rest of the course one under par to win. He needed another birdie, so he quickly got it with a brilliant iron shot at the par-five uphill eighth. Hogan narrowly missed a twelve-foot birdie putt at the ninth. But he was at the turn in 33 and three under par. He had to play the back nine even par to win his first Masters.

Many another had faltered before him amid the perils of the second nine at Augusta National. The eleventh, twelfth, and thirteenth holes had been nicknamed "Heartbreak Corner" with good reason. And playing cautious golf is no simple task. But Hogan proceeded to offer the thousands watching him a superb sample of finesse with the golf sticks. There would be no frills, few thrills, but a demonstration of control golf at its finest.

Coolly, carefully, Hogan moved the ball around the last nine holes. He was on the green in regulation figures at the tenth, twelfth, fourteenth, sixteenth, and seventeenth holes, two-putted for pars at each hole.

A branch of Rae's creek curls around the left of the green at No. 11, and Hogan always placed his second shot to the slope off the green to the right. "If you ever see me on that green in two," he said frequently, "it's because I mis-hit the shot."

He later lost a Masters when he thought he had to take chances and went for the green on the eleventh. This time, however, he played it to the right and chipped up to within four feet of the cup. He studied the putt longer than usual, then rolled the ball into the cup. On the 480-yard thirteenth, Hogan's drive placed him sufficiently well out that if he had chosen to do so he could have gone for the green with his second.

It appeared that he was going to do so, but he changed his mind and lofted an iron safe and short of the creek in front of the green. From there he chipped across and dropped the eight-foot putt for a birdie four. At the fifteenth, he also played short of the water with his second, pitched across, and two-putted for a par. Hogan knew all too well the price that could be paid if you popped your approach at the eighteenth too hard and the ball came to rest back of the hole on the upsloping green.

He deliberately underclubbed his second shot to lob the ball short of the green. Then he got down in a chip and a putt for his par. His 33-35—68—earned him the championship by two strokes with a total of 280.

"The final 18 holes was a classic in strategy and execution," Clifford Roberts noted. "Not a single one of those strokes would be called a missed shot or a mistake in judgment. And Ben made millions of golfers, and many others, very, very happy."

As Hogan was playing the eighteenth, Demaret walked up to Valerie standing with two writers. "Did you hear?" Demaret quipped. "Hogan had a twelve on eighteen and lost by six strokes!"

"I got a big bang out of it," said Hogan. "It wasn't so much winning the Masters. It was having all those people out there rooting for you—and then being able to come through for them. They're wonderful. I have had so much luck. If I never win again I'll be satisfied. I've had more than my share."

Yet, as with the U. S. Open, once Hogan won a Masters he threatened to make it an annual custom.

Ben's sentiment toward the Masters Tournament was illustrated prior to the 1952 event. He made arrangements to be host to a dinner for all previous winners. At that time he proposed the formation of the Masters Club, with its membership limited to Masters champions past, present, and future. Nine of the eleven who were eligible attended the dinner and voted in favor of Hogan's proposal. They also extended honorary memberships to Bobby Jones and Clifford Roberts.

In his book *The Story of the Augusta National Golf Club,* Roberts wrote of the Masters club:

Ever since its organization, attendance at the dinner has been remarkably good. In 1975, twenty-one of the twenty-two living Masters champions were present. Bob Jones never failed to attend as long as he was able to make the trip from Atlanta. I have never missed one of the dinners. Each year the new champion pays the dinner check, and receives as his certificate of membership a suitably inscribed gold locket in the form of the club emblem. The presentation is usually made by Ben Hogan or Byron Nelson. The dinners are always held on the Tuesday evening during the week of the Masters. Everyone wears his green jacket.

It was Ben's idea that the Masters Club meet annually merely for the purpose of enjoying each other's company. It was to be a time to reminisce, to hear Sam Snead's latest story, to dine well, and generally to promote good fellowship among members of the club. Over the years no one has been immune to banter and mildly sarcastic comments, including the management of the tournament. While socializing remains the dominant theme, the Masters Club has served some highly useful purposes.

Merely because of their identity, the members of the Masters Club automatically contributed to the development of the tournament. Their stature as players, and as men of character, has added greatly to the prestige of the event.

Equally important has been their active efforts in helping to make improvements. This applies to tournament procedures, tournament equipment, the golf course, player invitation regulations, course conditioning, and the designing of various facilities. A number of Masters champions are not only golf course architects or consultants but are students of engineering, agronomy, and horticulture.

I believe it is rather well known that the Augusta National has, from the beginning of the tournament, welcomed suggestions from all sources: golfing fans, patrons, players, architects and golf association officials. I also believe I can best explain my admiration for the members of the Masters Club by stating that they have probably provided more practical suggestions for improvements than the combined total from all other sources.

The first two years of the Masters Club Hogan was the host. "I discovered the tab for the dinner came to more than the winner's share of the purse," he said later. "So I finished second four times!"

That he conceived the idea of the Masters Club and was its founding motivation naturally gave Hogan much satisfaction and pride in the group through the years.

A key element in Hogan's usually masterful mix of mental and physical golfing characteristics was missing in 1952. He did not project the depth of determination and concentration. He was at times almost timorous in his putting. Not that the mechanics of the swing were affected all that much—he played some rounds of excellent golf. But he lacked the sustained drive of previous years.

Speculation as to the aftereffects of the accident gradually taking their toll, or a lessening of keen interest reducing his zeal, followed Ben throughout the year. He would win only one tournament.

Hogan did not compete in a tournament for ten months after the 1952 Open. He was busy moving to Palm Springs and becoming the head professional at the Tamarisk Club. The desert gave him new vigor, and he thought the turf condition ideal for developing his shots to their customary sharpness. He practiced regularly for four months before emerging for the 1953 Masters.

There were those who predicted he would regain his top form, but the majority opinion held that Hogan had lost something in 1952 and at forty years of age was not likely to regain it. Hogan was the first player to arrive at Augusta and start tuning his game. He now had the only lifetime Masters scoring average under par, 71.91 strokes per round in eleven appearances. But the stigma of a 74-79 finish of 1952 needed to be erased. And prior to the tournament Hogan made clear that was his primary intention. He said he was particularly ashamed of the 79 and was going to atone for it.

He recognized he was playing well in practice and thought the fairways were in near-ideal condition on the course. He could only wait to see how difficult the greens would be under tournament conditions. He had closed his putting stance slightly, and his confident stroke once again was in evidence in putting the ball. Hogan had the attitude of a man with a brisk purpose once more, more of a spring to his somewhat stiff-gaited step, and an air of authority that had been missing the year before.

Very probably Hogan could have accurately assayed his capabilities going into the 1953 Masters. He usually knew. They did not manifest themselves clearly to most observers until the second round. Hogan began with a 70, the noteworthy aspect of the round being that he required only thirty-one putts. That focused some attention on him. He was two strokes back of Chick Harbert's 68 and a shot back of Ed Oliver and Al Besselink with 69s.

That Ben's golf was forceful, his shotmaking brilliant, and his putting consistently fine became evident to all who watched his second round of 69. This time he putted thirty-two times, and his total of 139 led the tournament after thirty-six holes.

Not only were the personal elements functioning harmoniously for Hogan, but also the weather elements. Rain lashed the course the mornings of both the third and fourth rounds, but when Hogan's tee-off time arrived each day, so did the sunshine and calm. As the third round progressed, the chroniclers of the game started seeking superlatives to describe what they were seeing. One writer agreed with the fellow standing next to him as they watched Hogan score three straight birdies. "I'm going to leave," said the man, "because I don't believe what I'm seeing."

Oliver and Hogan, paired together, gave the Saturday matinee audience of the seventeenth Masters a classic shoot-out to rival any in the history of the game. Oliver set the tone of the two-man explosion with a birdie on the first hole, and the gallery hardly had a chance to breathe without gasping the rest of the way. Oliver shot a 34-33—67—but lost a stroke to Hogan's 32-34—66. Their best-ball tally was 31-29—60—over the par-72 Augusta National Course. Hogan had thirty-one putts.

At the fifteenth hole, Hogan dipped seven under par with a birdie while a group of professionals followed the pair's progress on the scoreboard upstairs in the clubhouse. One of the men stirred in his chair, rose, and started walking toward the porch outside. "Where you going?" a friend asked. "We can at least go out," said the man departing, "and breathe the same air he does."

Hogan's 205 total was a fifty-four-hole record for the tournament and pushed him to a commanding four-shot lead over Oliver in second place. Everyone felt that Oliver at 209, Bob Hamilton at 210, and Harbert at 211 had only outside chances, at best, entering Sunday's final round. And when the wind-whipped rain yielded to a bright sun and gentle breeze for Hogan's trek through the pines, there was no longer a question of the outcome.

"There is little doubt that whatever the conditions Hogan would have done what was required of him," said Al Laney, veteran golf writer for the New York *Herald-Tribune*. "For this man, besides being one of the greatest golfers of all time, is a competitor without a superior in sports."

The only drama lay in the number of strokes Hogan would shave off the seventy-two-hole record of 279 first set by Guldahl in 1939 and matched by Claude Harmon in 1948. Hogan beat that by five with a closing 69, this round using thirty-three putts. Oliver, in the right place but the wrong year, equaled the previous mark of 279 but was second by five strokes.

Oliver's futility was exemplified in the last round. He tried to make a race out of it by getting a birdie four at the second and a birdie three at the third. But by the time Hogan later played the fourth hole, Oliver had gained nothing.

Hogan, paired with Byron Nelson, bent a four-wood second shot along the curving downhill left side of the second fairway, and the ball was never a foot off the pin as it came to a stop twenty feet beyond the cup. Hogan two-putted for a birdie four. He narrowly missed an eight-foot birdie putt at the third. Then, at the 220-yard fourth hole, Hogan rifled a three-iron tee shot a foot from the cup for a birdie deuce.

Hogan took bogeys at the par-three sixth and the par-five eighth, where he three-putted, and turning in even-par 36 had lost one of his shots to Oliver. On the back nine, however, Hogan picked up birdie fours at the thirteenth and fifteenth, then finished grandly with a birdie three at the eighteenth for a 33, a 69, and record total of 274. Oliver posted 35-35—70.

Hogan's four rounds of golf were nearer perfection than anyone could remember ever being played on a championship-caliber course. So flawless was the execution and so brilliant the results that one had to search to find any shadows darkening the effort. There were no blots, only a smudge here and there. He needed only 126 putts for the seventy-two holes, a very skillful exhibition on the large, undulating greens.

Even Hogan was openly happy with the performance. "It's the best I've ever played for seventy-two holes," he said. "The best four rounds of golf in a tournament I've ever had." Through the years, his opinion remained unchanged.

Roberts, the tournament chairman, felt more positive than Hogan about it. Roberts wrote, "Ben Hogan stated his belief that his record in the 1953 Masters Tournament represents his best effort. We think it was the best 72-hole stretch of golf ever played by anyone anywhere.

"The four days absence of wind, moderate speed of the greens, excellent fairway turf plus the warm temperatures all combined to provide ideal scoring conditions. Twice we experienced rain but on both occasions it ended and the sun came out just before Ben's starting time. A truly great golfer took full advantage of his opportunity by producing a perfection brand of golf on each one of the four days of play.

"Records in sports usually remain record accomplishments for only a brief period. But we are wondering if Ben's record score of 274 isn't likely to stand, if not permanently, for a long, long time."

Hogan's U. S. Open record endured for nineteen years before Nicklaus broke it at Baltusrol. Ben's Masters record lasted twelve years before Nicklaus beat it with a 271 in 1965.

Hogan had a solid opportunity to win the Masters in 1954,

although he was far from the scintillating shotmaking of his incredible 1953 tournament success. This time Hogan's putting was mediocre, and for most of the tournament his irons lacked crispness and accuracy. Yet he survived a remarkable surge by amateur Billy Joe Patton to tie for the title with Sam Snead.

A play-off was scheduled on Monday, matching the two leading players of the post-World War II period and, fans agreed, possibly marking the end of an era. So more than five thousand poured onto the course to run and struggle and jockey for vantage points to watch the two great rivals have at each other.

"Ben Hogan gave away less about himself than anyone I ever met," Snead recalled in discussing how he would look for something uncustomary about the opponent as a tip-off the man might be under duress. On the first tee, Hogan said, "Good luck." Snead replied, "Good luck, Ben."

"Then he froze," said Snead. "He went to work to take me apart, concentrating as he always did like there was nothing in this world but his ball and those eighteen holes."

Despite the relatively ragged play in the tournament itself, the play-off did, indeed, produce some excellent golf by Hogan and Snead. It was close and exciting. After nine holes they were tied with one-under-par 35s. At the tenth, Snead chipped into the cup from sixty-five feet away to go ahead by a shot. Hogan squared it at the twelfth. Snead took the lead again with a birdie four at the thirteenth. They parred the fourteenth and birdied the fifteenth. At the long par-three sixteenth across the water, Snead was away with a twenty-five-footer and Hogan was about eighteen feet from the cup.

Snead charged the ball more than usual and got it within about a foot. Hogan was five feet short on his first putt. "Ben had never duffed a putt so many ways since I'd known him," said Snead. "It was such a change from the usual that it made my skin prickle."

Hogan pushed the next putt just enough to miss by an inch. He took a bogey four, and Snead was ahead by two strokes. Hogan won the eighteenth hole with a par four, but Snead won the play-off, 70–71. Hogan had reached every green in regulation, Snead fourteen. Hogan shot par on fifteen holes, Snead ten. Snead took three bogeys and Hogan one. But Snead's five birdies to Hogan's three and thirty-three putts to Hogan's thirty-six proved the difference. Snead called it "one of the closest matches I ever played."

Hogan played sixteen complete Masters in the years 1940–60. His average score per tournament was 286.4 strokes. The average winning score of those tournaments was 282.0 strokes.

Hogan's average score for sixty-four rounds was 71.6 strokes, and his average score per hole for 1,152 holes was 3.98. He shot thirty-four of the sixty-four rounds in par 72 or better.

Herbert Warren Wind, the golf historian, wrote in 1955: "In years to come, I am sure, the sports public, looking back at his record, will be struck by awe and disbelief that any one man could have played so well so regularly. . . . Ben Hogan, the outstanding sports personality of the postwar decade, has, to be sure, secured a place among the very great athletes of all time."

Ben Hogan's Record
THE MASTERS TOURNAMENT 1940–60

Augusta National Golf Club, Augusta, Ga.

1940   73-73-69-74—290   Tied for tenth

1941   71-72-75-68—286   Fourth

1942   73-70-67-70—280   Second (Tied for first, lost play-off.)

1943–45   No tournaments played.

1946   74-70-69-70—283   Second

1947   75-68-71-70—284   Tied for fourth

1948   70-71-77-71—289   Tied for sixth

1949   Did not play, injuries.

1950   73-68-71-76—288   Tied for fourth

1951   70-72-70-68—280   Winner

1952   70-70-74-79—293   Tied for seventh

1953   70-69-66-69—274   Winner (New Record by five strokes.)

1954   72-73-69-75—287   Second (Tied for first, lost play-off.)

1955   73-68-72-73—286   Second
1956   69-78-74-75—296   Tied for eighth

1957   76-75—Did not qualify (Cut of field at thirty-six holes began this tournament.)

1958   72-77-69-73—291   Tied for fourteenth

1959   73-74-76-72—295   Tied for thirtieth

1960   73-68-72-76—289   Tied for sixth

Complete tournaments played:	16
Hogan's average score per Masters:	286.4
Average winning score per Masters:	282.0
Hogan's average score for sixty-four rounds:	71.6
Hogan's average score per hole (1,152 holes):	3.98
Hogan's number of rounds, 72 or better:	34 (53%)

Figures do not include play-off rounds.
Figures do not include two rounds of incomplete 1957 tournament.

12

If there is anything more remarkable than Ben Hogan the golfer, it is Ben Hogan the man/The Reverend Granville T. Walker, 1953

Ben Hogan the man reaped handsome rewards from the success of Ben Hogan the golfer, but along with the profits were certain penalties. Personal privacy, which he guarded zealously, became increasingly difficult to maintain.

    Hogan learned that the axiom "Everybody loves a winner'' was not entirely accurate. More and more he was the target of verbal potshots from fellow tournament golfers and people connected with golf in other capacities. Not all, but many, of the barbs were based on misquotes or misunderstanding.

In 1952 a wire service story quoted Byron Nelson at length on his ''jinx'' over Hogan in match play. Ben met Byron in the nineteenth hole at Colonial Country Club in Fort Worth and asked him what kind of record book he was keeping, showing him a newspaper clipping of the story. Nelson read it and said, ''I certainly didn't say those things, Ben.''

Later, Hogan told a writer, ''I didn't think all along that it was Byron. But I think I know who was responsible for it.'' Another man had fed the quotes to a reporter as having come from Nelson.

These incidents became common during Hogan's reign over professional tournament golf—someone putting words in somebody else's mouth. Ben became cautious about even the casual locker-room remark, fearing that in the cold, black ink of print it might be misinterpreted. Hogan formed strong opinions of the various golf writers, and there were those he trusted and those he did not.

One year at the Masters Hogan was sitting talking with reporters when one he was wary of asked a question. Ben could almost fuse the discs of a writer's spine with his cold gaze, and after glaring at the writer for a moment he dropped his head and studied the floor. The other writers shifted from one foot to another in the awkward silence.

Gardner Dickinson, Jr., then a Hogan protégé, witnessed the scene and afterward asked Hogan, ''That was a very simple question—why did you embarrass the guy?''

''Well, I know him,'' replied Hogan, ''and I was just trying to visualize what kind of headline that guy's paper would get out of what I would answer.''

To a serious question, Hogan often gave almost the same thought he did a golf shot. And he was outspoken at times. When Max Faulkner, then British Open champion, issued a call for a match with Hogan in 1951, Ben told Clifford King of the Fort

Worth *Star-Telegram* sports staff, "Why, that would be like me challenging Bing Crosby to a singing contest, wouldn't it?"

Then there were those instances when he remained silent even though an answer or explanation seemed appropriate. In 1951 benefit matches were to be played in Charlotte, North Carolina, for Skip Alexander, a popular professional golfer who had been badly burned in a plane crash.

Hogan was scheduled to play, and when he did not appear the expressions of outrage were plentiful. Hogan made no statement, and not until a Fort Worth golf writer printed the information did anyone know that Hogan's plane had circled Charlotte for two hours but was unable to land because of bad weather and had to return to Augusta, Georgia.

In 1952 Hogan as the U. S. Open champion played in the first National Golf Day event, which was called "Beat Ben Hogan Day." Golfers throughout the nation could pay a dollar and with their handicap try to beat Hogan's score over the Northwood Club course in Dallas, where the Open was to be held. Hogan received $1,500 for playing the round and was criticized again when he did not contribute the fee to the National Golf Foundation.

Hogan did not respond, and a year passed before the Fort Worth golf writer who belonged to the same church as Hogan found out and wrote that Ben had brought the check to Fort Worth and endorsed it immediately to the church.

Then, through the Professional Golfers' Association, Hogan released the information with the statement, "I think charity is a personal affair."

One could not fault his reasoning, but the seemingly unnecessary refusal to speak out and quell the criticism was exasperating to writers who covered Hogan. Then, in a turnabout, Ben might seek out a writer and invite him to the locker room for a lengthy discussion on a similar issue.

This happened near the conclusion of a rhubarb in 1953 which involved Hogan, Lloyd Mangrum, the Las Vegas Tournament of Champions, and officials of the Pan-American Open in Mexico City. It started with a story out of Las Vegas that quoted a

Tournament of Champions official and a PGA official anonymously, and Mangrum indirectly. Their comments were critical of Hogan for refusing to play there after requesting a $5,000 guarantee and being rejected. The story said Hogan had asked the same amount from the Pan-American and received it.

Pan-Am officials denied that Hogan was receiving a $5,000 guarantee, and one said that Mangrum, Cary Middlecoff, and Jack Burke withdrew from the Mexico City event "only due to internal politics against one of the world's greatest players. Mexican golf fans can only believe that they're afraid and jealous of Hogan."

Mangrum was later interviewed about his role in the affair by a Fort Worth writer, and said nothing in the case "has caused Hogan and me to be any unfriendlier than we ever were. I've always been friendly with Ben until the past two years or so, I guess, but we haven't had much to do with each other. But, then, Hogan doesn't have much to do with anybody.

"Any argument between a sponsor and Hogan or any other players isn't my business, but I do know that Ben's never done anything to help his fellow pros. But that's all right. Maybe we've never asked him. Still, he hasn't gone out of his way, either. There is one thing I'll say for Hogan. He's going to end up with a lot of money, that's all."

Two weeks later Hogan asked the same writer to listen to his side of the story, but he would not be drawn into any argument with, or criticism of, Mangrum.

"The whole thing was so idiotic," said Hogan, "it wasn't even funny. I hated to have it come up because it hurt the feelings of the Mexican people and Mangrum, and it wasn't good for golf in general. If they had asked me earlier [at Las Vegas] I'd have been delighted to play there, especially since it was in aid of the Damon Runyon Cancer fund. Apart from that I'm a free man living in a free country. I don't like being told where I have to play and where I can't play. If I have to take orders as to where I can or can't play, I suppose I might as well go to Russia. And that's where they got it all wrong in the first place; I never did ask them [Las Vegas] for $5,000."

There were other golfers, both tournament and club professionals, who shared Mangrum's sentiments about Hogan, and most did not hide their feelings. And Hogan, complex and contradictory and keeping his own counsel, did not go out of his way to combat his detractors.

"I've been criticized for not playing in this tournament or that, or for demanding appearance money or guarantees, by the same fellows I'm helping," he said. "They don't realize that every time I raise my exhibition fee or the amount of appearance money, it's helping all professional golfers. An exhibition fee of $1,000 was unheard-of until I got it. But you'll notice that when I raise mine, others do the same, and the young fellows coming up in the future will be able to demand more because we've raised the level."

As he added one major victory after another and became the top gate attraction in golf in the early 1950s, Hogan was not the least bit reluctant in pushing the price to the limit the market would bear. He became less tractable in golf and other business deals and was a tough negotiator. He always said no to the first offer, and he was often uncompromising, unyielding, and uncooperative.

Sometimes this attitude led him to extremes. Once, after a tournament round, Fort Worth television sportscaster Bud Sherman asked Hogan for a couple of minutes' interview for his evening sports program.

Hogan turned and asked, "Is your program sponsored?"

"Why, yes," said Sherman.

"Then how much will the sponsor pay me to appear?" Hogan shot back.

"But it's a news program!" Sherman protested as Hogan walked away.

His best friends and most loyal backers encountered difficulty in explaining or justifying that kind of behavior to critics, yet within twenty-four hours Hogan might reverse his field and graciously consent to a number of similar requests. An employee of the Ben Hogan Company once said, "Hogan will give you the shirt off his back one day, but he might want you to return it the next."

He told Jack Murphy, who wrote a *Collier's* article about

him, that "the next time I'll make the thousand dollars." But two years later he insisted despite objection by the editors of *The Saturday Evening Post* that the writer collaborating with him on a first-person story about his 1953 successes be given half the magazine's $5,000 fee for the story.

Hogan's stature and his knowledge of the game made him a desirable source of opinions, and writers continually sought comment from him about other golfers. He rarely consented. If he said anything at all, it was usually complimentary and reflected his keen analytical ability.

When Babe Zaharias died, a Fort Worth writer called Hogan and asked for a comment. The reply was unexpectedly complete and revealing of Hogan's knowledge of the famous woman athlete and golfer.

"She dominated women's golf because she had strength, willpower, the desire to win and she worked hard on her game," Hogan said. He recalled the first time he had seen her, and other details. Then he added, "I think the best way to describe Babe is that she turned out to be a diamond. As we all know, a diamond is a piece of coal that's been hard-pressed for many years."

As that description of Babe Zaharias illustrates, Hogan's intellect gave him an excellent verbal descriptive ability, and he was an interesting, pleasurable person for off-course conversations. Those few who got to know him well enjoyed his colorful relating of experiences, his wit and easy sense of humor. Despite the general impression, Hogan laughed with slight provocation, and if it was at himself he laughed louder than usual. Jimmy Demaret's wisecracks about Hogan found their most appreciative audience in the butt of the quips.

Another who sparked Hogan to witty repartee and pleasure was Tommy Bolt, the supposedly irascible golfer with the reputation for club-throwing and ill temper. They had a good time on or off the course, with Hogan claiming Bolt swung the golf club like Dracula and Bolt retorting that if Hogan could swing like he could, he'd win the Open sometime.

These were two guys who supposedly did not enjoy playing golf; it was a grim business with them. Once they were playing a round with Ted Gwin, then professional at River Crest in Fort Worth, and Raymond Gafford, professional at Ridglea in the same city. Before teeing off, Gwin, a big muscular guy, was taking some practice swings and Hogan said dryly, "Boy, if I could swing like that, I'd go on the tour."

On the back nine of Colonial Country Club Hogan and Bolt began playing "call" shots, which meant each would designate which club was proper for the next stroke. At the par-three sixteenth, Hogan said it was a four-iron and Bolt argued it was a five-iron. By this time, Gwin and Gafford were laughing at the Bolt-Hogan antics so much they had almost quit playing seriously.

Hogan hit a four-iron shot from the tee, and the ball landed and stopped about three feet from the cup.

"See, I told you," said Hogan.

"Yeah," rejoined Bolt, "but you hit it fat!"

"Well, it called for a fat four-iron," Hogan replied.

"You have to give Ben a chance," said Bolt, "that's all he wants. He's the friendliest guy in the world, but most of these guys either don't want to believe it or they're scared to approach him."

Hogan did not have many relationships among professional golfers like he had with Bolt. Those few who did get to know Hogan well discovered a man of sincerity, honesty, religion, and friendship, all of such depth that they did not surface readily nor could they be probed easily.

Whitney Martin, for many years a top sportswriter with the Associated Press in New York, offered another insight into Hogan.

"He seems to me like a guy who wants to be friendly, but he won't make the advances. I think, perhaps, because of an inherent timidity. I think he's a very likeable person as just Ben Hogan, and that's the way he wants to be friendly. He could throw out his chest and say 'I'm Ben Hogan the great golfer' and force himself on the world in many ways. But he doesn't. I've seen him at an airport where they didn't recognize him. He'd stand back and let folks crowd him in their hurry to get to the baggage counter, when just one word of his identity would have given him top priority on service."

Marvin Leonard, wealthy Fort Worth merchant, oilman, and sportsman who founded Colonial Country Club, was an early sponsor of Hogan and became his close friend, adviser, and business associate.

Leonard loaned Hogan $250 when Ben set out on one of his early tries at the tour and told Ben to pay him back when he could. A few months later Hogan telephoned from San Antonio to tell Leonard he had the money and was mailing it to him.

"I told him to forget it," Leonard recalled. "Just the fact that he'd worked and scraped along to save that money, which was a lot in those days, in just a few months and wanted to pay me back was payment enough for me."

Ben's decision to join a church typified the analytical approach he made to any major move—he wanted his decision to be based upon the proper motive. The Reverend Granville T. Walker was pastor of the University Christian Church across the street from Texas Christian University in Fort Worth, and Dr. Walker was an eloquent, interesting, and learned speaker. No doubt his personal appeal was a factor in the church's popularity and growing membership.

"We went several times," Valerie said, "but Ben was hesitant about joining because he feared he would be joining because of the man, Reverend Walker, rather than what the church stood for. Then one day Reverend Walker preached a sermon on just that subject and explained it all so well that Ben said after the service on the way home that he'd found out for sure that it was the church he wanted to join."

Early in 1952 a Fort Worth golf writer offered Hogan a golf ball and asked if he would autograph it for his daughter's first birthday, and Hogan did so. At the 1953 Masters, the writer stood with Valerie and watched Ben putt out on the final hole to complete his record-shattering score of 274 for seventy-two holes. Then the writer went to the press tent and called his office to alert the sports desk that the story would be longer than usual.

When the writer reached the second floor of the clubhouse, the press conference with Hogan was already under way. Writers were crowded around Hogan, seated on the leather-cushioned shoe-locker bench. The late arrival stood on tiptoes to look over the shoulders and get a glimpse of Hogan as he answered the questions.

Somehow, Hogan spotted the writer and interrupted the questioning with one of his own. "Anybody got a pen?" he asked, looking around. Will Grimsley, big redheaded Associated Press writer, handed Hogan a pen. Ben pulled a golf ball from his pocket, signed his name on it, looked up, called the Fort Worth writer's first name, stretched out his hand, and said, "Here, this is for your daughter."

One aghast writer asked, "Is that the ball you just finished with?" Hogan nodded and said yes.

Hogan had remembered the request and signing of the ball more than a year before, and obviously had given it enough thought to conclude that his signature on just any golf ball was inadequate.

And this was the man who had a few minutes earlier completed the best four rounds of tournament golf he had ever played and considered by Clifford Roberts and numerous others the best four rounds *anyone* had ever played.

After that amazing performance in the 1953 Masters, the clamor began for Hogan to compete in the British Open for the first time. The May 1953 issue of *Golf Monthly* published in Edinburgh, Scotland, had an article headed, "Hogan, the Master—Come Over," and read, in part:

The man who was shattered to the verge of death in a motor smash, who fought back from an encased body lying rigid for months in a hospital, to win the American Open championship thrice in the last five years, and has again won the Masters Tournament, is becoming a legendary figure to the golfers of Britain.

Carnoustie, did he come and triumph, would impress the seal on Hogan's fame. In phantasy we see Hogan, the enigma, silent, austere, resolute, battling out on the windswept links of the Angus seaboard, one of the massive tests of the game in the whole world of golf. Do not leave it too late, Ben, to take your place amongst the immortals of golf and the supreme honour in the game. Scottish golfers, and especially Carnoustie, whose sons did so much for golf in your homeland, will take you to their hearts.

Soon after winning the Masters, Ben said to Valerie, "I think I'll enter the British Open if I win the U. S. Open."

"I should think you'd want to play in the British Open if you didn't win the U. S. Open," Valerie said.

He kept delaying the mailing of his entry until the deadline of June 6 neared, and the U. S. Open was still to be played when he did file his entry.

"And I knew when I mailed it," he said, "that I'd go to Scotland whether I won my fourth U. S. Open or not."

13

The man who could play for glory better than anyone I've ever seen is Ben Hogan./Byron Nelson, 1956

Ben Hogan was forty years old and playing the finest golf of his life in 1953. Thus the timing appeared to be perfect for his first and only attempt to win the British Open.

Not since Willie Park in the initial event in 1860 had a golfer won the British Open on his first try, and as well as he was playing, Hogan knew there was no guarantee of victory accompanying his entry.

"I began to feel a pressure that I've never before experienced about a tournament," he said. "You know, a great many people have built up in their minds a mythical Hogan who wins whenever he wants to win. Well, it does not work out that way. That's just not true.

"I found myself in a situation of proving I was as good a golfer as those who had won the British Open before me. As you get older you find yourself having to prove yourself again—and it eats on you. I think golfers would last longer and win more if this wasn't so.

"Every place you go you're expected to play excellent golf, often super golf. It's awfully hard to do that, but people won't accept less."

Even as these thoughts occupied his mind, and the pressures built, Hogan won his fourth U. S. Open at Oakmont, his score of 283 beating Sam Snead by six strokes. Then Ben focused his attention on the British Open.

Bob Harlow, whose career as PGA tournament director, players' agent, observer, and writer of golf spanned back to the 1920s, was editor of *Golf World* magazine, and his story of the Open at Oakmont included these words:

"If additional evidence was needed to prove that Hogan is the golfer of the decade and the golfer of the century he provided the details at Oakmont. . . . Four out of five Opens may not be as spectacular as a grand slam, but for accurate play against the toughest fields it looks like the top achievement in competitive golf."

Harlow, referring to other players' complaints about Hogan, wrote, "The fact is Ben just beats the hell out of the other players and naturally this does not improve his opponents' morale."

At Oakmont, discussing the forthcoming foray to Scotland, Hogan commented that perhaps he would need some long underwear because of the cold weather on the east coast of Scotland. And Ben said it might be more comfortable if he could find some cashmere "long handles." Especially since his accident,

Hogan's patched-up body and redeveloped golf game suffered from cold and damp weather.

The week after his comments, Ben received a wire from Abercrombie & Fitch, the New York store that specialized in equipment for sportsmen. The telegram informed Hogan that the store had cashmere long underwear and that he would be unable to find the item in Scotland.

The price was ninety-five dollars a pair. Hogan telephoned Paul Shields, a well-known yachtsman and good friend in New York City, and asked him to order two pairs of the underwear and have them delivered to the hotel where Ben and Valerie would be staying in New York en route to Scotland. As it developed, Hogan could not wear the "long handles" because they were too warm. He eventually kept one pair for hunting trips.

When news of his possible need for the underwear spread, well-wishers and other firms began sending unsolicited gifts of the garments to Hogan.

"Why, I kept getting underwear sent to me," he said, "until paying duty on them almost broke me."

Ben Hogan could have come up with many excuses for bypassing the British Open of 1953 and his stature in golf this side of the Atlantic would have been unaffected. The only way he was going to gain in Scotland was by winning. Hogan was not afraid of losing—he had learned to live with that years before.

What concerned him was that if he did not win, the people in Great Britain would think, "Well, the American players aren't as good as they are supposed to be." These thoughts added to the pressure. Weighing all factors, it would have been an easy decision to stay home.

He had several reasons for going. He was determined to prove to himself that he could play the different course and weather conditions and maneuver the smaller British ball. He also was aware that Carnoustie was one of the toughest courses in the world.

"I'd heard so many comments that had come secondhand to me that people didn't believe I could play under those conditions," he said, "and I was somewhat determined to prove that I could. In that respect, I think that's been one of my driving forces because over a period of years people have said I couldn't do this and I couldn't do that, or I couldn't play different type shots that are called for on a certain kind of course.

"Even at Colonial, my home course in Fort Worth, I heard several times that I couldn't win this year because I wasn't a very good wind player."

The wind was twenty-five miles per hour steady with gusts up to forty miles per hour every day of the 1953 Colonial National Invitational, and Hogan shot 282 to win by four strokes.

A third, lesser, reason for Ben's decision to enter the British Open was the standardization of golf rules achieved in 1952. The British under the uniform rules now permitted use of the center-shafted putter after having banned it for many years. Hogan used a center-shafted putter with a brass blade made from a melted-down doorknob during World War II.

The prize money certainly was no incentive for Hogan to play in the British Open. The purse had been increased, but first place was worth only $1,400. Cary Middlecoff, later discussing his first effort in the British Open, remarked, "Under the present setup over there you go over to play just for the glory. You have to finish first to make ends meet financially, and there's no glory in finishing second. No one remembers the runner-up. It's tragic, but that's the way it is."

Ben, as nonplaying captain, and Valerie had gone to England in 1949 with the United States Ryder Cup team. All travel arrangements and accommodations had been made for them on that trip, and food from the United States was shipped to England for the players and their wives.

This time the Hogans were responsible for arranging their own travel. They planned to fly to Prestwick on the West Coast, drive across Scotland to Carnoustie, spend three weeks there, go to Paris for a week's vacation, then take the ocean liner S.S. *United States* back to New York. The National Cash Register Company offered Ben and Valerie lodging in its guest house at Dundee, eleven miles from Carnoustie.

Hogan thought about having enough meat and vegetables

for three weeks frozen and shipped over, but he recalled that the English resented the Ryder Cuppers doing that in 1949.

"So I didn't do it," he explained. "I didn't want to have the papers or someone raise a stink about it."

Ben had started playing the Titleist golf ball even before severing connections with MacGregor Sporting Goods, and the Acushnet Company, makers of the Titleist, geared up and produced dozens of British-size golf balls for Ben to use at Carnoustie. The British ball weighs the same as the United States ball, 1.62 ounces, but at 1.62 inches is .06 of an inch smaller in diameter. The difference in figures is minute, but the difference in distance, especially in a heavy wind, is enormous.

Lloyd Mangrum and Frank Stranahan, the fine amateur who always played well in Great Britain, were two other Americans entered in the British Open. It was to be Mangrum's first bid, too, although he was generally overlooked in the excitement of Hogan's entry. Personality differences seldom took precedence over respect for another's golfing skill among the top American professionals, and Mangrum was no exception.

When Ben departed New York for Scotland, Mangrum said, "If I can't win I hope Ben Hogan does. This would be a great thing for Hogan, who has won all of our major titles in this country."

When they first arrived at Prestwick, and for a few days after that, Ben and Valerie had difficulty understanding the Scottish brogue and the wording of questions. Ben consented to a press conference upon arrival at Prestwick. One man acted as spokesman for the reporters.

"He'd ask something and I wouldn't know what to say," Ben related. "I'd have to think for five minutes to figure out what he meant by his question because they didn't word them the way we do."

The spokesman asked Hogan if there was any special significance to the tie he was wearing. Ben did not know what he meant by that, either. Hogan glanced down at his tie and said no. Then the spokesman pointed out that Ben was wearing a tie of red, white, and blue colors.

Ben rented a Humber automobile and hired a chauffeur,

John, who drove the Hogans across Scotland and remained in their service until they departed three weeks later.

When Hogan first saw Carnoustie, one of the "Stone Age" Scottish courses dating back to the birth of the game, he quickly understood why no golfer had ever won the British Open on his first try (Bobby Jones ran into so much trouble in the 1921 British Open he dropped out in the third round). The course was a drab-looking mixture of browns and faded green colors with no trees. It looked to Ben like land that had never been developed since the year one.

"They just go out and seed a tee on the level ground and then seed a green the same way. In between they mow the grass for a fairway," Ben described his impression, "and that's the way the course has been for two hundred years, and I suppose, will be for two thousand more. They put bunkers in like a man throwing rice at a wedding. It looks like they took a handful of bunkers and threw them out over the course. Where they landed, there are bunkers.

"You never have a level lie. One time I'd be hitting with a baseball swing and the next time way down beneath my feet. Every fairway is rolling and full of mounds. There are no trees. I'd guess they mow the greens once a week, maybe, and the fairways once a month. Usually they let goats in on the fairways and they never touch the rough."

Hogan planned his schedule to permit two weeks of practice, play, and familiarization with both the Carnoustie course, where the championship would be contested, and the shorter Burnside course, where one qualifying round would be played.

Hogan came off the eighteenth green of his first practice tour of Carnoustie with misgivings. The fairways were hard and pockmarked with divot holes. The greens were hard, but heavy and slow where they appeared to him to be faster. This upset his putting rhythm and also forced him to play more hit-and-run approaches instead of flying the ball to the green. There were many blind shots to the greens and very few landmarks on the course by which distance might be calculated.

It was completely different from the "target golf" of the United States, where the courses have boundaries, or borders, of trees, fences, and hedges, the fairways are easily distinguishable from the rough, and the greens usually well defined by surrounding trees, bunkers, or ponds. Often, when Hogan stood on the tee at Carnoustie and looked down the course, he could not tell where the fairway ended and the rough began.

Furthermore, the ground jarred his wrists when he tried to hit through the ball and the turf with his irons, and he realized he would have to make an adjustment for that. All in all, the 7,200-yard duneland course close to the Firth of Tay and the North Sea did, indeed, loom as the "monster" he had heard it called. So Hogan set about reshaping his game to the demands of the course.

In Hogan, the Scots found a match for their brusqueness. He told them about the greens: "You can't putt on putty." Another time he said, "I've got a lawn mower back in Texas, I'll send it over."

The Scots, proud of old Carnoustie, replied in kind with the suggestion that champions had always been able to adjust to their course. And that was what Hogan planned to do as he practiced in the mornings and played the course in the afternoons. On three of the days he only hit practice balls and did not play a round. He was having trouble getting used to the distance he could hit the smaller ball.

He kept taking about two clubs less—say, a seven-iron instead of a five-iron—than he would with the American ball and then hitting so hard that the ball quite often rolled over and beyond the greens. Each day's problems had him asking, "What am I doing here?" Hogan decided early that the tee shot would be the most important because of the type of course and the weather, and the necessity to keep the ball out of the heather and gorse.

"If you hit that rough," he said, "you're going to go for a 77 every round." Ben did not even practice hitting shots from the heather and gorse in the rough because he believed that anyone whose ball landed there did not have a chance to win the tournament anyway. So he practiced much more with his woods than he normally did for United States tournaments. On his practice rounds he hit three balls from each tee, one down the left side of the fairway, one down the middle, one down the right side—no mean feat in itself. He was learning not only how to negotiate the bunkers in the middle of the fairway but which positions offered the best approach to the greens.

Hogan played several practice rounds, however, before he learned that he was not hitting from all of the back tees that are used in the championship. They were far back in the gorse and heather, and he had not found them. The championship tees are called tiger tees, and Ben guessed the reason was that only tigers would frequent such areas. The tiger tees increased the length of the course from the standard 6,701 yards to 7,200 yards.

Hogan solved the problem of the bone-jarring turf and sand-filled divot holes by picking the ball off the ground much cleaner with his irons than he normally would. He decided there was only one solution to his inability to judge distance. Nearly every evening after dinner—it did not get dark until about eleven o'clock—he walked the Carnoustie course, often in reverse, eighteenth green to the first tee. He memorized the hazards, undulations, bunkers, and shape and slope of the individual greens. In addition, in practice rounds he memorized what club was required from various places on the fairway, taking the weather and other factors into consideration.

He never got to the point where he trusted himself to look and judge whether he had a four-iron shot or not. But he did trust his memory.

The Scots, some of them walking five or six miles to play a round in the twilight after closing their shops or completing their day's farm chores, came to admire this solitary figure intently studying their course. They began to call him the "wee ice mon," and they recognized that he was a stern man for a stern game.

Sterling Slappey, an Associated Press writer, was following Hogan on a practice round when he struck an approach shot to within a foot and a half of the cup on a hole. Two elderly Scots were watching at the edge of the green.

"Och, 'twas a great iron shot," said one, pulling on his pipe.

"Aye," his companion replied, "and he left himself only a wee putt adjacent."

Hogan was being exposed to some customs quite different from those in United States golf as he continued his preparation for the British Open. It surprised him that the pin placements on the greens were unchanged throughout the two weeks of practice and the qualifying rounds. The cups were then moved for the start of the tournament but remained in the same position for the four rounds of competition.

He made several inquiries about registering for the tournament and obtaining credentials, but no one could tell him the procedure. On the day before the tournament he received a letter in the mail with his ticket and a guest ticket for Valerie, plus the pairings for the qualifying rounds. This was the only communication he had from tournament officials, and, in fact, he never saw an official of the British Open until the last day of the event.

The first qualifying round was scheduled for Monday, July 6, and Hogan played the shorter Burnside course. Hogan, who could not work up a keen competitive pitch for qualifying rounds, scored a 70 at Burnside and a 75 the next day at Carnoustie and easily made the list of one hundred qualifiers. Also in the field was a truly international cast including Bobby Locke, the defending champion, Peter Thomson of Australia, who was to win the tournament the following three years, Roberto DeVicenzo and Antonio Cerda from Argentina, and Mangrum and Stranahan from the United States.

Dai Rees from Wales, Henry Bradshaw and Fred Daly from Ireland, Eric Brown, Hector Thompson, and John Panton from Scotland, and a large English delegation headed by Max Faulkner, a former titlist in the event, were among the British Isles representatives. Observers were terming it the finest British Open field of modern times as the tournament proper got under way on Wednesday.

The weather was cold and windy, and there was occasional hail as the players trudged Carnoustie in the first round. In his practice rounds Hogan had never hit more than a light eight-iron second shot on the first hole. In the tournament's first round, because of the wind at his face, he nailed a driver and two-iron as hard as he could and did not reach the green.

Hogan felt all right about his play in scoring a 73 in the first round because of the wind and the bounce-and-run shots he had to make. He was not satisfied with his putting, however, and he was worried about his energy. He had been losing weight since February, and had lost weight through the two weeks of practice at Carnoustie. The meal rations were small and the food, in his words, "awful," and he tried to keep his strength by eating a great deal of fruit.

Those familiar with Hogan's hard-to-please eating habits could scarcely believe his getting along on lamb chops or mutton and the same three vegetables every day for three weeks and being served roast beef sliced as thin as boiled ham only twice in that period. He would not touch the kidney pie.

The 73 left Hogan three strokes back of Stranahan going into the second round, where Hogan once again could not drop his putts although he played well and scored a 71 for a thirty-six-hole total of 144. This was two shots back of the coleaders, Rees with 72-70 and Brown with 71-71. DeVicenzo was at 143, and Hogan thought the powerful Argentinian's tremendous distance off the tee might have everyone else playing for second. De-Vicenzo might have run away with the tournament if he could have avoided trouble. Stranahan and Peter Thomson were at 144 with Hogan. Locke and Faulkner were at 145.

Hogan's caddy was Cecil Timms, who had been recom-mended by two United States amateurs, Harvie Ward and Dick Chapman. Timms was a good caddy, treated Hogan's clubs like the crown jewels, kept his shoes shined, but may have made his greatest contribution by relieving some of the tension that Hogan naturally was experiencing.

Timmy, as he was called, was so nervous that Hogan found it necessary repeatedly to stop and talk to him and calm his caddy. On long putts the caddy would hold his head down bet-ween his arms and refuse to look. On other putts Timmy might growl fiercely at the ball, make faces, jerk his arms about wildly, and adopt various postures of "body English." Hogan never asked a caddy what club to use but if he picked a five-iron and the ball was short of the green and he commented that he should have taken more club, Timms would say, "I had me hand on the four-iron."

Hogan was walking well ahead of Timms once when a rain squall hit, and Ben stopped, waiting for his caddy to hurry up with the umbrella. When Hogan looked back, Timms was busy putting on his rain suit, and by the time he came up with the umbrella Ben was soaking wet.

Hogan carried fruit drops in his golf bag each day to eat for energy. He doled out some to Timmy and said they were for the caddy but that he would need the rest. On the second round Timmy ate his share and Hogan's too. Ben bought some more and told his caddy to leave them alone. But soon they were all gone, and Hogan lectured the caddy sternly that he must leave the next jar of fruit drops alone. "But Mr. Hogan," Timms said, "I could eat them all day they're so good."

Hogan, susceptible as usual to inclement weather, had a touch of the flu by Friday morning and took a shot of penicillin before going to Carnoustie for the final thirty-six holes. He had other medicine but did not take it for fear of getting an upset stomach.

Carnoustie was crowded with more than twenty thousand people who had come from all over Scotland to watch this legendary golfer make his run at their championship. And back in the United States, not since D-day of 1944 had the public been so unanimously interested in an invasion of foreign soil. Golfers, golf fans, and people who did not know a driver from a putter were following Hogan's progress. On the final day they telephoned newspapers and radio stations by the hundreds of thousands. Radios were turned on in homes, automobiles, drugstores, barbershops—everywhere—to catch the announcers who were giving almost hole-by-hole accounts of Hogan's play.

Although not wearing the long underwear, Hogan was bundled in more clothing than normal on the final day, which offered a mixture of cold winds, gray skies, occasional rain, and some sunshine. On his morning tour Ben had an excellent round going with a reading of four under fours, a 68 for eighteen holes, moving to the seventeenth hole. There, however, he shoved his second shot into a trap by the green, made a mediocre recovery, then three-putted for a six. It was the only six he had in the tournament. He got his four at the eighteenth for a 70 and after fifty-four holes was tied for the lead at 214 with DeVicenzo.

The latter also had a bad hole in scoring a 71 for his total of 214—he hit one out of bounds at the ninth hole. Hogan and DeVicenzo were one stroke ahead of Rees, Peter Thomson, and Tony Cerda. Hogan had a number of players to worry about during the break for lunch.

Valerie brought lunch for Ben and herself and a thermos of coffee and told Timmy to take Hogan's lunch to him in the locker room of one of the small clubhouses across the street from the course. The caddy was gone for a while, and when he returned to Valerie he sat around watching her eat. She began to feel sorry for him and asked if he would like to share her lunch. Timms ate about half of Valerie's sandwiches, and not until later did Valerie and Ben compare notes and discover that the caddy had been given half of both their lunches.

"So he ate a full lunch while Valerie and I each ate half a lunch," Ben said.

When the field was tightly bunched as it was entering the final round, Hogan always had contingency plans in case it was necessary for him to take chances, and he always knew exactly which holes were the most conducive to any alteration in his pattern of play. Fortunately, DeVicenzo was playing six to eight holes ahead of him on the afternoon's concluding eighteen, so keeping track of the Argentinian would be relatively easy. Rees and Thomson also were ahead of Ben, but Cerda was behind him, and Hogan recognized the smaller Argentinian as a serious threat, too.

Hogan started with consecutive fours on the first four holes, and his pretournament summation that 283 would win the tournament was at least within range. But a friend informed him that Cerda had birdied the third hole, and Hogan thought at the time he needed to shoot a 70 or within a stroke of that to win.

He wanted to get a couple of birdies somewhere, and the first one came in such an unorthodox manner that the adrenaline pumped through Hogan stronger than ever, the surging victory mood erased all thoughts of weariness or illness, and the British Open championship was practically decided. That first birdie came at the fifth hole, a slight dogleg to the right measuring 388 yards.

Hogan was now hitting the small ball up to 300 yards off the tee, and he cleared the bunker in the fifth fairway with ease. He played his approach to the side of the incline of the green, which was double-terraced and stretched about forty to fifty yards in length. The ball hit about eighteen feet from the pin, but then rolled back off the green and stopped in the edge of a trap, about half in the sand and half out, caught by a couple of blades of grass.

Hogan did not like chipping out of sand and described it as the hardest shot in the world for him to make. But he was fearful of trying to blast out and risk sending the ball over the green. With his right foot in the sand, his left on the grassy bank, he chipped the ball with a nine-iron. He picked up the ball cleanly and sent it scurrying upslope toward the cup. The ball skipped across the grass, banged against the back of the cup, bounced into the air three or four inches, then fell with a rattle into the hole for a birdie three.

"As luck would have it," said Ben of the shot, "I hit it just right."

The skillful, yet fortunate, stroke put Hogan one shot ahead of Cerda and three ahead of DeVicenzo, who had made the turn two over with a 38. Hogan was in the lead for the first time in the tournament, and he brought to bear all of his inner reserves to press the advantage. At the sixth hole, playing much longer than its listed 521 yards, he zapped two whistling wood shots to the edge of the green and birdied with a four.

Parring the next three holes, Hogan turned two under par with a 34 and learned that Stranahan and Rees were in with scores of 286 and that Thomson was not likely to do better than match that. Par in would give Hogan 284, so he was now interested in holding what he had and keeping track of Cerda behind him.

At the tenth hole, as Hogan was taking his stance on the tee, out of the corner of his eye he saw a dog walk across the tee about ten yards in front of him. He waited and thought he saw the dog walk into the crowd. But just as Ben hit a full driver the dog walked back across the tee. Hogan's ball missed the dog by about two inches. He went on to par the tenth, eleventh, and twelfth holes. Then he spanked a five-iron tee shot 175 yards to the green at the thirteenth and rolled home a twelve-foot putt for a birdie deuce.

He learned DeVicenzo had finished at 287 and that Cerda was back at even par after a five at the twelfth, when his ball struck a spectator. Hogan was certain after the thirteenth that he had the championship if he did not do anything foolish on the finishing holes. He parred the next four holes, and as he teed off on the eighteenth, the seventy-second of the tournament, the fairway was lined along its 450 yards with fans seven to ten deep. His drive was perfect, and his approach split the green, the ball stopping some twenty feet from the pin. He two-putted for a birdie, a 34 in, a 68 and a 72-hole score of 282. The 68 was a new single-round record for Carnoustie, and the 282 was a record by eight strokes under the previous competitive best over the course.

Hogan, who had forsaken his usual lightweight white cap for a warmer wool one, removed his cap, tipping it to the applauding crowd. The attitude of almost caustic skepticism that he had first encountered around Carnoustie had changed to one of warm admiration and friendliness.

An old Carnoustie caddie told Timms, "It's no' possible, but it's a fact."

Valerie was unable to see Ben's finish because of the crowds, but her thoughts were about his health. She insisted that John, the chauffeur, bring Hogan's coat, and she made sure he put it on before walking out to receive the championship cup. Fatigue was evident on Hogan's face.

In the United States Hogan's feat was considered a national triumph, and millions thrilled to his performance. "Wonderful, simply wonderful," said Bobby Jones. "I'm delighted that Ben won it. Under the conditions, it was a marvelous accomplishment." "There you are," said Byron Nelson. "He's eight strokes better than anyone else who ever played it for seventy-two holes. I know he had his heart set on winning it and I'm sure glad he did it.''

Britain's sportswriters unleashed every superlative. "Hail the greatest golfer of our time," said Morris Peden in the London *Daily Herald*. "And who shall say he is *not* best of all time?" wrote Leonard Crawley in the London *Daily Telegraph*. Crawley was a British Walker Cup star prior to World War II, and he said the final rounds of 70 and 68 showed that Hogan had the "indefinable quality of being able to bring himself to his peak when the pressure is the greatest."

Fred Pignon of the London *Daily Mail* had seen all of the golfing greats from Francis Ouimet through the years to Hogan. "Ben Hogan is the greatest golfer America has ever sent to our country," Pignon said, "as every knowledgeable person in Scotland believed. It's indisputable that he's the best. He's streets ahead of all of them.

"You know, we don't call our Open the British Open, it's *the* Open. We consider it a world's championship, and it would have been grossly unfair had Ben not won it. He's the finest player of a golf shot I've ever seen. Not only does he possess skill to make a shot with a minimum of error, but he also has mental command, mental control, under stress where most golfers of equal skill do not.

"For example, the odds against any golfer getting down from the edge of the green in two might be ten to one. But if it's Ben, the odds are ten to one he will get down in one and a half, if he has to do it."

"All in all, it was hard to imagine a victory which could have been more completely victorious," golf historian Herbert Warren Wind wrote. "Perhaps that is why it had scarcely been achieved when it began to have the ring of a legend to it. . . . Since he had never entered a British Open before and since it was probable that he would never do so again, what had happened— his arrival in a strange land, the perfect completion of the task he had set himself, his succinct departure—seemed to be sealed off from all other events, suspended as it were, in a separate and somehow unreal land of its own, so that if it were not known for a fact that there had been a 1953 British Open on that remote stretch of duneland in Forfarshire, you might have thought that the whole story was the concoction of a garret-bound author of inspiration books for children who had dreamed up a golfing hero and a golfing tale which he hoped might catch on as had the exploits of Frank and Dick Merriwell in the days before golf was considered the proper vehicle for the dreams of glory of the red-blooded American boy.''

Hogan, who came to believe the tee shot is the most important in golf, was in the rough only one time in 108 holes, and that was in a qualifying round. He completely avoided the Barry Burn, the creek that runs around and across portions of the Carnoustie course before flowing into Carnoustie Bay. His was a superb example of preparation and execution.

Hogan did not putt really well the entire tournament and left the ball short of the hole frequently the first three rounds. And throughout the seventy-two holes he never once bounced an approach shot "stiff" to the pin. "You'd think in that many holes I'd luck at least one up close, wouldn't you?" he commented. He maneuvered the ball expertly, however, and his organization and management more than compensated for the putting problems.

Although Stranahan was in contention all the way and tied for second, Mangrum was never a factor in the tournament. He finished nineteen strokes back of Hogan with a score of 301.

Hogan's triumph climaxed the greatest year any golfer had experienced since Bobby Jones in 1930. His "Triple Slam," as it came to be called, of Masters, U. S. Open, and British Open was the closest to Jones's "Grand Slam" yet achieved. Hogan entered six tournaments and won five of them, the lone blemish a tie for third in the Greenbrier Invitational.

He won the Masters, Pan-American Open in Mexico City, Colonial National Invitation, U. S. Open at Oakmont, and British Open at Carnoustie. Over five of the toughest tests of golf in the world, his winning scores were 274, 286, 282, 283, and 282, an average of approximately 281 per tournament. His average eighteen-hole score in the five tournaments was 70.35 strokes, or 3.92-plus per hole.

His winning totals in the three major championships—the Masters, the U. S. Open, and the British Open—were course records. Including four pro-amateurs, Hogan won $20,313.99 in 1953. A golfer today who won the Masters, Colonial, U. S. Open, British Open, and a tour tournament comparable to the Pan-American would win at least $175,000, so much have the purses increased.

The British Open was Hogan's ninth major championship and his sixth since his 1949 automobile accident. His two PGA titles were won at match play, but in the four U. S. Opens, two Masters, and British Open victories Hogan averaged 281.3 strokes per seventy-two holes.

Hogan was not sanctimonious, nor a hypocrite, but he said after the British Open, "I don't think anybody does anything unless the Lord's with them. I think it's fate, and supposed to be, that I won these tournaments; otherwise, I wouldn't have won them. All of those victories required more guidance than one human being can give another and I've been fortunate enough to receive that guidance. I think the Lord has let me win these tournaments for a purpose. I hope that purpose is to give courage to those people who are sick or injured and broken in body as I once was."

The U. S. Open triumph at Merion in 1950 would always be prized the most by Hogan because it proved to him that despite the accident and the lasting damage to his legs he could still play major championship golf and win. But for the sheer joy of triumph, the British Open ranked first.

"The British Open gave me my greatest pleasure," he told Jim Trinkle of the Fort Worth *Star-Telegram* years later. "Certainly the others were pleasurable, but none of them gave me the feeling, the desire to perform, that gripped me in Scotland."

There were more years and more tournaments and more challenges ahead, but Hogan's conquest at Carnoustie would stand through the years as the grand climax to the implausible career of an improbable champion.

14

We are proud of you not only as a great competitor and as a master of your craft, but also as an envoy extraordinary in the business of building friendship for America. Best wishes to you and Mrs. Hogan./President Dwight Eisenhower, 1953

New York City's homecoming celebration and ticker-tape parade up Broadway were the first for a sports figure since Bobby Jones's return from England in 1930, and the enthusiasm of golfers and nongolfers alike reflected how Hogan's triumph had captured the imagination of Americans.

Valerie was travel-weary and Ben was still thin from the loss of weight, yet both were relaxed, looking refreshed and exhilarated at reaching their homeland.

He and Valerie were in the salon of the S.S. *United States* in the entrance to New York Harbor when they were besieged by reporters and photographers at 5:30 in the morning on Tuesday, July 21, 1953. The news media party of fifty had been transported out from Pier Nine aboard a Coast Guard cutter and entered the ocean liner through a door amidships near the waterline. As they entered the salon, each was welcomed by Valerie and Ben.

Both were pleased to learn that rain had been falling in Fort Worth and West Texas, where there had been a severe drought for several months. As tugs began nosing the liner into the harbor, the Hogans animatedly answered questions, posed for news photographers, and submitted to filmed newsreel and television interviews.

Though they had been alerted to the media invasion of the ship and the schedule of the homecoming celebration, Valerie and Ben confessed to being overwhelmed by all the commotion, or "fuss" as Hogan called it. "I can't imagine people getting up so early to do this for us," said Ben. "People are wonderful."

"He is thoroughly exhausted," said Valerie. "I would like to see him not try for any more big championships if he has to work as hard as he did for these. I would rather he started playing golf for fun."

Hogan announced that he planned to start a club manufacturing company and would take an active role in management. He said it would not interfere with his competitive golf and he was certain he would play in the U. S. Open again. He did not commit himself to another British Open.

"I play golf because I like it and any time I enter a tournament I try to win," he said. "But so far as trying to beat someone's record, I don't go for that. Sure, anyone would like to win five U. S. Opens, or one Open. I'd like to win a fifth Open; I'd like to win ten of them."

Asked his reaction to the smaller-sized British golf ball, Ben replied, "It goes like a bullet and you can hit it a mile. If we used it on our greens, they'd be shooting in the fifties. There wouldn't be any such thing as a par-five hole."

The Hogans were outside the salon on the sport deck in the early-morning sun participating in newsreel interviews when the liner passed the Statue of Liberty. Hundreds of commercial vessels and private boats dotted the waters in welcome to Valerie and Ben.

Helicopters whirled overhead, the many tugs, police launches, and fire department boats sounded their horns in a cacophony that drowned out the interviews, then the fireboats shot streams of water high into the air in salute. When the liner passed the West Forty-sixth Street pier, those aboard saw large "Welcome Hogan" banners.

The Hogans were given a twenty-mile ride around the city to the start of the official parade. Fifty motorcycle policemen escorted their two open limousines. Along the route thousands of people cheered and waved. Shirtless factory workers, white-collar office workers, and others stopped work, leaned from windows, and yelled "Hi, Ben! or "Hi, Champ!" as the cars passed.

The crowd along the Broadway route was estimated at 150,000, and thousands more crowded office windows. Hogan, sitting atop the back seat, waved first one hand and then the other. He did not recognize a single person among the thousands and seemed somewhat disappointed that he had been unable to spot anyone he knew. Troop A and Troop B of the Mounted Squad of police and the fire department band and color guard formed the rear guard of the motorcade.

In the ceremony on the steps of City Hall Mayor Vincent R. Impellitteri said as he presented a citation to Hogan, "Here you are, the world's greatest golfer and I am probably the worst." In 1930, when he introduced Jones in a similar ceremony, Mayor James J. Walker said, "Here you are, the greatest golfer in the world, being introduced by the worst one."

The official citation for distinguished and exceptional service lauded Hogan for being a great champion "whose achievements as an outstanding sportsman are an inspiration to the youth of the nation." Impellitteri read a telegram from President Eisenhower, then the mayor said, "More than the eyes of Texas were upon you in that British Open. We watched with devotion and excitement. . . . Ben, you have set up three marks for everyone to shoot at, a mark of ability, a mark of personality and a mark of sportsmanship.''

The "wee ice mon," as the Scots fondly called him, melted visibly under the warmth of the welcome. The golfer who never choked on the golf course did so now.

"This is the hardest course I've ever played," Hogan, his voice quavering, responded. "I'm so grateful that I can't explain it in words. This sort of thing brings tears to my eyes. I have a tough skin but a soft spot in my heart and things like this find that soft spot. This tops anything I've ever received. I don't think anything can surpass what's happening now."

Hogan's selection to the PGA Hall of Fame was announced; he was the thirteenth golfer to be named and the first of his era.

Valerie and Ben bounced back quickly from the hectic Tuesday, and their animation on Wednesday evening as they regaled guests with stories of their experiences during the British Open would have surprised those who always thought Ben was cold and grim. Valerie would start a story and then begin laughing and Ben would pick up the telling, or the reverse order would occur.

"Over there," said Ben, "the caddies drop the bags on the greens when you get ready to putt and when the hole is finished the people just walk right across the greens. Kids and dogs, they let everybody and anything on the course; more dogs than you ever saw. The people would come from everywhere to watch. Ladies with a small child on each arm would drag them the full eighteen holes. They'd bring babies in baby buggies and push them the full eighteen holes. They'd bring their lunches and stay all day.

"Rain doesn't bother them. They just put on rain suits and keep playing or watching. And when a strong wind and rain comes across the course, they squat down under their umbrellas, like rabbits or chickens, you know, until the rain and wind quits, then they'd get up and go on—darnedest sight you ever saw."

The Scots' devotion to golf, their pride, their hardiness, and their friendliness impressed both Valerie and Ben. They thought the galleries were among the most knowledgeable and polite that Ben had ever played before, and he felt most of the people were pulling for him to win on the final day of Carnoustie.

Cecil Timms, Ben's caddy, had provided most of the laughs for them. Ben said that after Timms had caddied for him about five days in practice, he still had not made a firm commitment to hire Timms for the tournament. Timms went to the chauffeur, John, and asked if "Mister Hogan" had said anything about hiring him as his tournament caddy. John said "Mister Hogan" had made the remark that he was not very satisfied but that he was going to give Timms one more chance.

This so unnerved the caddy that in the afternoon Hogan told Timms he could be his caddy through the tournament.

Valerie and Ben alternated in telling how Hogan played the first tee of the Burnside course for his first official round of the British Open, the initial qualifying round.

"I walked up to the tee box and all I saw was a woman sitting off to the side in a little house," said Ben. "The twosome in front had teed off and when I thought it was about time I walked onto the tee. Still, nobody had said anything about how or exactly when I was to tee off. The twosome in front had hit their second shots and gone on so I teed up my ball but the people shook their heads and said no, they'd let me know when to tee off.

"So I waited, and an engineer drove his train up—the tracks ran right beside Number One fairway and I'll bet half a dozen trains went by while I played the hole. Then I hear this *beep-beep* on a little horn. That's all, and someone said that's the signal to tee off. I looked around and it was the women in the little house. She'd blow this little horn *beep-beep* and you'd tee off. When she blew the horn, the people lined all the way down the fairway nodded their heads in approval, signaling me that I could tee off now."

"I could see Ben was about to burst holding back his laughter," said Valerie. "It was all so new and strange to us but, of course, perfectly normal for them. And when that lady tooted that horn and those people nodded, it was all he could do to keep from laughing.''

The practice tee at Carnoustie was about a mile from the first tee, and Ben soon learned he could not practice there. ''You could play the first three holes to get there,'' he recalled, ''but it was an army shooting range, so help me. About two hundred yards off they'd be shooting machine guns and the bullets would make a loud noise when they went through the targets and hit the sand dunes. It wasn't conducive to good practice sessions, so I moved over to a more private area off the course. But the people would follow me everywhere to watch me practice and play.''

Ben said his mother did not think he should go to Scotland because she was afraid he would get sick. ''I did catch cold, a slight case of influenza, I guess,'' he added, ''but since my fortieth birthday something's always been wrong with me. I wake up every morning with a new ailment. I was complaining to Toots Shor about my aches and pains and he said only one word was needed to explain away my ailments. Age.''

Bobby Jones, now a semi-invalid, flew to New York City to attend the United States Golf Association dinner, a grand tribute in itself and one enormously appreciated by Hogan. The dinner was in a banquet room of the Park Lane, and famous people from other sports joined those of golf in paying homage to Ben. The comparisons between Jones and Hogan had been rekindled by Hogan's ''Triple Slam,'' and the words of Jones were eagerly awaited. Jones, once asked if he could have beaten Hogan, had a succinct reply: ''I don't know. I never played him.''

''I am not one who believes my era was the greatest necessarily because I lived in it,'' Jones told the dinner crowd. ''People today run faster, jump higher and run farther and it's only natural that they play golf better. Ben has pretty well proved that they can. But the thing that makes a champion is not necessarily precision play. The man who works the hardest wins the championships. Ben, with the game he has, will keep winning championships as long as he wants to badly enough.''

The presence of Jones, Sarazen, and other former U. S. Open champions greatly pleased Hogan. Francis Ouimet, the first

American-born golfer to win the American Open—in 1913—was there, and so was Fred McLeod, the 1908 U. S. Open champion.

"I weighed a hundred and eight pounds soaking wet when I won the Open!" McLeod told the audience. "How do you think I feel when they call this guy Bantam Ben?"

No golfer before Hogan had won the Masters, U. S. Open and British Open in the same year, and no golfer since has done so. Arnold Palmer in 1962 won the Masters and British Open, but lost a playoff to Jack Nicklaus for the U. S. Open championship. Nicklaus won the Masters and U. S. Open in 1972 but finished second to Lee Trevino in the British Open.

Trevino won the U. S. Open and British Open in 1971 but did not challenge in the Masters. Trevino with five major championships became the most successful Texas professional since Hogan.

15

By 1975 someone will come along they'll be comparing with Hogan, just as Hogan came along after me./Robert T. (Bobby) Jones, 1953

No one expected Ben Hogan to have another 1953 in him or to expend himself physically over the many months of preparation and participation the success of that year required. Yet he had played so superbly it was taken for granted that he would remain capable of winning for a long time.

A person who might have suggested that Hogan would not win another major championship and only three events in the remaining eighteen years of his competitive career would have been considered a heretic and probably beaten to death by other club members wielding sand wedges. Surprisingly, that is what the future held for Hogan.

He teamed with Sam Snead to capture the Canada Cup for the United States in 1956 in England, and Ben won the accompanying individual International Trophy. And in 1959 he won his fifth Colonial National Invitation. Those three boosted his total number of titles to sixty-eight, although in the official records of the Professional Golfers' Association, which include only PGA-approved or sanctioned tournaments, Ben is credited with sixty-two victories.

Not that Hogan's "touch" or talent evaporated; for several years he was often in contention. Bobby Jones had said that Ben would keep winning as long as he wanted to badly enough, and Hogan never lost his burning desire to win.

But there were other reasons. The aftereffects of the automobile accident intensified as he grew older; preoccupation with his club-manufacturing business caused cracks in his concentration; Ben's nerves were becoming frayed by the years of competition and this was reflected in a deterioration of his putting effectiveness; and he still suffered from a play-off phobia. The loss of his ability to putt was the major factor, and Hogan was frustrated by his helplessness in coping with it.

"It doesn't bother me, I've putted so terrible so much," he once said resignedly. "You get to thinking it's futile, all right, but I've gotten to the point where it surprises me when they go in."

Those remarks were made after he had played a tournament round in which he had sixteen putts for birdies, several of ten feet or less, and had not made one of them.

"If Dow Finsterwald had been putting for me," Ben said, "he would have been fifteen under par on the round."

His fellow professionals always touted Ben as one of the finest putters in the history of the game, but Hogan knew they were being facetious.

"That started as a joke," he said. "I thank them, but it's a joke. I used to be a good putter, back in 1938, '39, '40, and through '45, but from there on I've been a bad putter."

Hogan could pinpoint putting as costing him at least two additional major championships, and perhaps more, in the years after 1953. But he probably did not attribute his tribulations in play-offs to a phobia. He disliked play-offs intensely, not so much because of the extra physical demand but from a mental standpoint.

"You gear yourself mentally and prepare and plan for four rounds of the tournament," he explained once. "Then there's a play-off, and it's an anticlimax for me. I have a letdown and can't get back up for the play-off."

This was before television saturation and the sudden-death duels right on the heels of the seventy-second-hole tie which offered the combatants little opportunity to let down. They settle the issue in the modern era while the golfers' adrenaline still flows strongly from the final round.

Whether it was a phobia or not, play-offs were combined with poor putting when Hogan failed to win his third Masters in 1954 and his fifth Open in 1955.

In the play-off with Snead for the 1954 Masters championship Hogan reached every green in regulation figures while Snead hit fourteen. But Hogan needed thirty-six putts on the round to Snead's thirty-three and Snead won, 70–71. The pivotal point of the match, both agreed, was when Hogan three-putted the par-three sixteenth hole from about eighteen feet and yielded a two-stroke lead to Snead with two holes to play.

Snead was sensitive to remarks that first Nelson, then Hogan, had his "number," and that the two Texans had won five U. S. Opens while he had never won the major championship of this country.

"All I know is that it's true Hogan and Nelson won plenty of tournaments which I didn't," Snead said, "But any time Hogan and I met in a head-to-head play-off, I won. We met three times over the years when we were rivals. The score reads: Snead 3, Hogan 0."

Hogan won several tour events in play-offs, and the victory he cherished above all others was achieved in a play-off. That was the 1950 Open at Merion, where he tied Mangrum and George Fazio with his great par at the finishing hole, then beat them in the next day's shoot-out. The tournament was the most meaningful of all to Hogan because it proved to him that despite the accident injuries he could still play championship golf and win.

Even so, the much-publicized losses to Nelson in the 1942 Masters, Snead in the L.A. Open and 1954 Masters, and Fleck in the 1955 Open took precedence in the memories of most people, and on balance Hogan became known, and would be remembered, as a poor play-off performer. And amateur psychologists speculated as to whether Ben's psyche bore the scars of that play-off experience with Nelson when the two were fifteen-year-old caddies at Glen Garden.

While putting and play-offs were frustrating him, Hogan took pleasure in a golf development that could not be measured in scoring figures or recorded in won-lost columns. The golfing President, Eisenhower, and the golfing king, Hogan, were inspiring the biggest explosion of interest in the game that had ever occurred in the United States.

Mark H. McCormack, in his 1968 edition of *The World of Professional Golf,* offered many of the modern-era circuit golfers a brief but hard-hitting lesson in history.

"I have one sharp word of sermonizing for the pros of the U.S. tour, especially the younger ones," McCormack wrote. "They are getting rich right now on the work of other men, some great ones who, comparatively speaking, never made vast sums from their lifetimes in golf: Walter Hagen, Gene Sarazen, Byron Nelson, Sam Snead, Ben Hogan, Jimmy Demaret. They are the personalities who captured the public, they made pro golf a successful sport in this country, and they did it when you had had a big year if you made $10,000, when you traveled four to a car, or two to a trailer, and you took up an invitation to dinner with the club members because, by George, that was one meal for sure you wouldn't have to pay for."

Bob Harlow, editor and publisher of *Golf World* magazine, ranked Hogan as "the golfer of the century." Since the century was only in the beginning years of its second half, most observers did not go quite so far as Harlow, although at the time most who undertook to rate golfers placed Hogan at the top of the list.

Dick Metz, whose career as a player spanned the years from Bobby Jones to the 1950s, said, "They're really concentrating on teaching now, coordinating the teaching ideas, and ten years from now the group will come up that'll be the best ever. Age doesn't always determine the bracket, or era, of a golfer. Ben, for example, was just as good a golfer in 1932 as in 1942, and if I had to pick the greatest golfer, I'd pick Hogan, for the simple reason that he had a little bit more in every department, particularly in judgment and determination. If he were playing in the Po-Do Open, he'd try just as hard as if he were in the U. S. Open. That's his edge."

Pint-sized Paul Runyan, who was a rarity in that he gained great respect both as a tournament player and as a teacher, also bridged three competitive decades. He won the PGA championship in 1934 and 1938, and his eight and seven victory over Snead in the latter is the record margin for a final. And Runyan once beat Hogan in a PGA match.

Runyan rated the various players on the basis of their skill with each of fourteen clubs. He placed Hogan first with the two-iron and nine-iron and had Ben in the top four in proficiency with six other clubs. As a result, Runyan ranked Hogan first among the ten greatest players of all time, with Jones second and Hagen third. And he ranked Hogan first among the ten greatest contemporary golfers, with Snead second and Mangrum third.

By the time Toney Penna undertook to rank the golfers in 1965, three of those great players whom Jones, Hogan, Metz, Demaret, and others had foreseen were picking off major championships in clusters. They were Jack Nicklaus, Arnold Palmer, and Gary Player.

Penna, who signed Hogan to the MacGregor Sporting Goods advisory staff in 1937 for $250, rated the players' ability with sixteen clubs, awarding ten points for perfection, nine for second, and down the scale. He awarded fifteen points each for the ultimate in concentration and aggressiveness and ten points for the maximum in positive thinking. A perfect score under his system was 200 points. The lowest score Penna gave in any category was a 6, to Jones with the eight-iron and Tommy Armour with the pitching wedge and sand iron.

Among the several 7s Penna distributed was one for Nicklaus with the sand iron, one for Byron Nelson with the putter, and one for Sam Snead in positive thinking.

Only with the two-wood, four-wood, one-iron, nine-iron, and putter did Hogan receives less than a perfect score, and he had no rating below an 8. But his 189-point total placed him third on Penna's all-time top ten, behind Nicklaus with 193 points and Jones with 192. Palmer was fourth with 188 points. While interesting as a method of ranking, Penna's list like the others proved nothing and only caused lively arguments among the partisans of each golfer named.

The big surprise of Penna's list was his giving five others the same perfect score in concentration as Hogan.

As the game's popularity soared, so did the sales of the Ben Hogan Company's golf clubs, and in every year of operation the demand exceeded the plant's capacity for supply. Hogan spent much of his time supervising the plant, striving for improved manufacturing machinery, designing clubs and testing them personally. This cut sharply into the hours he formerly spent on the practice tee.

Hogan and his stockholders sold the Ben Hogan Company to American Machine and Foundry Company in 1960, and the financial stories reported the transaction was for $3 million in AMF common stock. Hogan remained as chairman of the board and chief operating officer and continued his personal supervision of the company's design, manufacturing, and testing processes. His approval was necessary for every detail, including newspaper and magazine advertisements.

And that was the year, of course, that Hogan made his last strong bid for a fifth Open title at Cherry Hills in Denver. After his return to Fort Worth, a friend was consoling him on the failure at the last two holes, and Hogan replied, "Hell, I played with a kid who should have won it by ten shots!"

The "kid" was Nicklaus, twenty-year-old U. S. Amateur champion who looked up to Hogan more than any other golfer and was playing with him for the first time in a pressure-packed final thirty-six holes of a U. S. Open.

"That was the first time we played," Nicklaus recalled in 1977, "and Ben was always very nice to me. After we played at Cherry Hills every year he'd come to me and ask me if I'd like to play; I played with him several times at Augusta and before U. S. Opens. I enjoyed playing with him. I learned a lot from him. I didn't learn that much on the swing—he was built and played so much differently than me. Still, it was just such a pleasure to watch him play. He was always very courteous."

In the company of Hogan at Cherry Hills, and in contention to become the first amateur winner of the Open in twenty-seven years, Nicklaus displayed remarkable composure. He scored 69-71, led the tournament at one point in the final round, and eventually finished second at 282 to Palmer's 280.

Hogan knew golf talent when he saw it, and he recognized in Palmer and Nicklaus the wave of the future washing over him.

16

I think we are so fortunate in the game of golf today that we had people [like Hogan] in the past who put the game first. Otherwise, we'd be in the same situation all these other sports are./Jack Nicklaus, 1977

Bobby Jones retired at twenty-eight with thirteen major champ-ionships; at age twenty-seven Jack Nicklaus had won nine major titles; and Arnold Palmer won six by the time he was thirty-three. Ben Hogan was a few months shy of his twenty-eighth birthday when he scored his first victory in a tour tournament and was thirty-four when he gained his first major crown, the 1946 PGA at Portland. He was almost forty-one when he won the last of his nine major championships in 1953.

Hogan's career was cockeyed in chronological comparison to those greats before and after him, and crammed into too few years to suit him. While there were no tournaments played in 1943, Hogan was in the service and missed 1944 and much of 1945, leaving the Air Corps in August to play in eleven tournaments, five of which he won.

But the automobile accident in February 1949 put the most severe crimp in Hogan's career. Not only did it knock him out of action for a year when he was at the top of his game, but the damage to his legs forced him to curtail his tournament schedule.

Hogan averaged winning ten-plus tournaments per year in 1946, 1947, and 1948, and in those three years and the first month of 1949 scored thirty-three victories. From 1950 on he entered only about half as many tournaments as he had been winning annually prior to the accident.

Small wonder, then, that in conversations through the years Hogan in looking back might let a note of bitterness surface. When he did, however, he quickly caught himself and was almost apologetic about it.

Once, after mentioning that he might have won more tournaments and more money if it had not been for the time he missed, Hogan told the Associated Press's Deene H. Freeman, "Everybody is always wanting five years more. Please, let's not make a big thing out of my leg injury. I've been lucky and I wouldn't want to do anything over again differently."

Another time, when observers were questioning why he was undergoing the punishment of practice and tournament play (Byron Nelson said, "I don't know what he is trying to prove"), Hogan explained, "Time's runnin' pretty short if I don't play now. I enjoy practicing and playing in tournaments. Besides, I haven't really done what I wanted to do."

Someone asked what he meant. "I haven't won enough tournaments," Ben replied.

So even as he suffered through the sixties from his leg and shoulder ailments and his putting, Hogan remained the "perpetually hungry" golfer. There would be no more victories, but there would be applause at every green, many times a standing ovation, as spectators demonstrated their sincere admiration of a great champion. And for one short stretch during the decade, the masterful Hogan "touch" would miraculously return, and many who had never seen him in his prime would marvel at his golfing skill.

But before that, Hogan relinquished center stage to Palmer, then to Nicklaus. As Hogan reached the twilight of his career, Palmer arrived as the greatest boon to golf since steel shafts. The foundation of tournament golf that Hogan, Snead, Nelson, Demaret, and their contemporaries had laid was there. Palmer built upon that foundation the modern, mushrooming structure of professional tournament golf; Nicklaus came along to keep house, and television added the stained-glass windows.

Palmer and television coverage of golf may not have happened simultaneously, but it seemed that way. Palmer had all the charisma Hogan did not. Palmer was not a stylish golfer nor artistic shotmaker; he was a slugger who usually appeared to be overpowering a course. His "army" of followers not only numbered in the thousands wherever he played; through the wonders of the TV tube they numbered in the millions in the nation's living rooms.

People identified with Palmer. He was a warm human being, and he made errors like human beings do. He became synonymous with the word "charge!" Palmer might whack the ball a prodigious distance into the rough, behind the trees or bushes, or into trouble of some other kind, but when he came striding purposely off the tee, animated as always, his legions would be electrified with anticipation. They knew that whatever was necessary, be it hitting the ball left-handed with a putter or slicing or hooking around an obstacle, their man would figuratively stampede the ball into the hole, and quite often for a birdie.

"Palmer was the big gun as far as getting the tour to where it is today," Gene Littler said. "He was the most charismatic player ever. He did everything the public wanted him to do."

Palmer's meteoric sweep across professional golf's history lasted only six years where major championships were involved, primarily because of a recurring problem with his right hip, but also because Nicklaus had turned professional and quickly set about challenging Arnie's supremacy.

Between them they won six of the first seven Masters of the 1960s (three each), but in other major events they had to share honors with Littler, Billy Casper, Gary Player, and several other fine golfers.

One of those quirks of fate peculiar to tournament golf, such as Snead and the U. S. Open "jinx," befell Palmer. While twenty-one different players won the PGA championship in the years 1950–70, Palmer was not among them. He finished second three times, and it was the lone major title to elude him.

Hogan, Demaret, and most members of their era could only look wistfully at the burgeoning prize money on the PGA tour, a reflection basically of the interest ignited by Palmer. In forty years the total prize money on the tour grew from $134,700 in 1935 to $7,839,750 in 1975.

Snead, however, crept in occasionally to grasp a slice of the riches, and this did not surprise Hogan.

"Why, Sam and Julius Boros are just in their prime," Ben commented. "A good swing will last forever."

Nicklaus did not tarry in showing signs he might very well be the golfer whom Jones, Demaret and Hogan had in mind when they forecast someone would come along to compare with Ben. Jack had power, and he had accuracy along with distance off the tee; he was close to Hogan in his ability to concentrate; he had classic execution of the golf swing; and one had to be pretty "picky" to say he was weak with any club. He was, to top it off, an excellent putter. Nicklaus also was quite similar to Hogan in the capability to plan and manage.

In the late 1960s Hogan said, "If you can manage, you don't have to be the world's greatest golfer. You need to organize yourself mentally and physically. If a man is keen enough to maneuver the ball right and left, if he's sharp enough, it makes it so easy to win you can damn near run away from them. You strive for an edge, then management will hold that edge for you."

Nicklaus was a fervent disciple of that view. He added the 1962 U. S. Open to his two Amateur crowns, then in 1963 scored his first Masters and PGA triumphs. Even with this early burst into prominence, however, few were quite prepared for what Nicklaus did at the 1965 Masters.

Hogan was in the field, and his record of 274 in the 1953 tournament was still considered "unassailable" by most observers. Nicklaus shot 67-71-64-69—271—to beat Ben's record by three strokes and second-place finisher Palmer by nine. Hogan was twenty strokes back in a tie for twenty-first.

Nicklaus won the Masters again in 1966, then in 1967 became the first defending champion to miss the cut. And although Gay Brewer won the tournament, that Masters, the twenty-fifth and last of Ben's career, became a surprise showcase for the old Hogan magic as he turned the silver anniversary appearance into one of the golden moments of golf and his life.

Ben's golf generally was good, if a bit strained, in those years, especially so for a man of his age and ailments. He was fifty-four, and his left shoulder was shot full of medicine—he had three operations on it the next two years—at the 1967 Masters, yet he caressed the ball for a 74-73 in the first two rounds and made the cut. In the third round on Saturday Ben matched par of 36 on the front nine.

Somewhere, somehow, as Hogan walked from the ninth green to the tenth tee, someone switched on the time machine and turned the dial back fourteen years. He shot a record-tying six-under-par 30 on the back nine for a 66, the lowest round of the entire tournament. The only other 66 he had scored at the Masters was in the third round of the 1953 event when he had set his record of 274.

"The course was a little faster in '53," he said, "and I think I played a little better then than I did today."

Hogan struck a seven-iron second shot at the tenth hole, and the ball nestled down seven feet from the pin. He sank the putt, and the stunning streak was started. At the eleventh his six-iron second put the ball a foot from the cup for a second straight birdie. At the tricky twelfth, his six-iron tee shot dropped the ball fifteen feet from the hole, and he hovered over his putt for a long time before stroking the ball into the cup for a third straight birdie.

At the par-five thirteenth, Hogan whipped a four-wood second shot to within fifteen feet of the hole and two-putted for a fourth birdie in a row. He parred 14, and by then the scoreboards around the course had carried the message, the growing crowd was in full cry and the clubhouse sofas were emptied as players and fans flocked to see this miracle in progress.

Hogan reached the fringe of the green on the par-five fifteenth with a driver and four-wood, then got down in two for a fifth birdie. He parred 16 and 17, then before most of the estimated thirty thousand people he rolled in a fifteen-foot putt for a sixth birdie at the eighteenth hole. The applause that had been rolling over him at every green reached a crescendo at that final green.

The cheers that greeted almost every weary step and each of the thirty strokes were loud, but laced with reverence for the old warrior. Hogan later rated that round as the second-greatest thrill of his career, next to the 1950 Open.

"I received an ovation at almost every hole," he said. "It made you feel very humble for people to appreciate what you were doing."

Hogan told Gene Roswell of the New York *Post,* "I am still embarrassed to get before people and putt. Hell, I'm even embarrassed to putt when I'm alone, but the only way to beat this thing is to play. I hear children and ladies saying, 'For God's sake, why doesn't he hit it faster?' So I say to myself, 'You idiot. You heard them. Why don't you hit it faster?' "

Mark McCormack recalled that the night before Hogan

shot that 66 Gary Player was bemoaning the way professional golf does not let you stay on top, that the golfer is forced to prove himself a champion constantly or the awards, the fame, and the recognition will be claimed by someone else.

"I walked by the practice tee today," Player told McCormack, "and there was Ben Hogan practicing. The great Ben Hogan. And do you know, not a single person was watching him, not one. I don't want that to happen to me."

But the morning after the 66, when Hogan was on the practice tee as usual, there were spectators.

The third-round Masters performance—Hogan shot a 77 the fourth day and finished tenth—was the biggest hurrah but not the last remaining for Hogan. The next month in the Colonial National Invitation Ben shot his best four rounds of tournament golf of the decade with 67-72-69-73, and until the lapse on the closing holes of the fourth round was within a stroke of the lead. His 281 total tied him for third, three shots back of winner Dave Stockton.

Stockton said he had learned a lot of golf just by following Hogan and watching him play. "Right now," Stockton commented during a round at Colonial, "I'm sure you could find several players in Hogan's gallery."

Hogan did not congratulate Nicklaus after the latter's record performances in the 1965 Masters and 1967 Open. "Never had a word," said Nicklaus. But years later Hogan was generous in praise of his successor.

"Golfers today are better than in my day, and there are so many more of them," Ben said once. "Then, too, players are bigger and stronger today. It's like all swimming records are being broken, and they still are swimming in water. Nicklaus is one of the greatest, who doesn't have any faults that I could recognize. His main attribute is that he is a tenacious competitor."

One facet of Hogan's life that few ever realized—and he definitely did not want publicity about it—was his effort to help others, especially golfers, who suffered some injury or illness— as he had—that jeopardized their careers or future enjoyment of the game. Numerous times Hogan either by letter or in person sought to bolster the spirits of these people, and one example illustrates what his efforts usually meant to them.

Gene Littler underwent an operation to remove malignant tumors in 1972, and there was the natural concern as to whether he could ever resume his fine tournament career.

"Ben did one really nice thing for me," Littler recalled a few years afterward. "He sent me the nicest letter and gave me words of encouragement that really helped me. I was sure pleased to hear from him."

Ben, his swing only faintly resembling that of his great years, made a final competitive effort in 1971 when he entered the Champions tournament at Houston. He was nearing his fifty-ninth birthday but just had to keep trying. And while his farewell was unpleasant for him and had overtones of sadness for everyone else, perhaps it was appropriate that the inevitable occurred on a golf course.

Playing the first round on a strength-sapping humid day, Hogan yanked three, three-iron shots from the fourth tee into a ravine about 175 yards away. He staggered from the green with a nine on the par-three hole and finished the front side with a score of 44. He took a double bogey at the tenth and a bogey at the eleventh, and was eleven strokes over par. At the twelfth hole Hogan drove it down the fairway, then rapped his approach shot to the green.

As if he had at least convinced himself he could still hit a couple of decent golf shots, Hogan called it a day and a career. He stood with hands on hips, white cap squared above a stoic countenance, as his caddy walked around the pond to the green and picked up the ball. Hogan told his playing partners, Charles Coody and Dick Lotz, "I'm sorry, fellas," and took a cart back to the clubhouse.

When a writer asked him a few years later if he would ever play competitive golf again, Ben replied, "After the way I played that day, I didn't think an announcement was necessary."

The golfer had already come along to break two of his records; the golfer would probably come along to match his triple crown of 1953; the golfer might emerge to match or exceed his four U. S. Open championships; the fame and recognition, as Gary Player had lamented, were being passed on to succeeding generations of golfers.

But thousands upon thousands of people who had thrilled to his golf shared the sentiment so simply, yet eloquently, expressed by Bernard Darwin, the most eminent of England's golf writers, who was seventy-six years old when he watched the 1953 British Open at Carnoustie, Scotland:

"I am happy to have lived long enough to see Ben Hogan play golf."

TOURNAMENTS WON by BEN HOGAN

1938/Hershey Four-Ball

1940/North and South Open
    Greensboro Open
    Asheville Open
    Goodall Round Robin
    Winner: Vardon Trophy, 423 points
    Leading money winner: $10,655.00

1941/Miami Four-Ball
    Asheville Open
    Inverness Four-Ball
    Chicago Open
    Hershey Open
    Winner: Vardon Trophy, 494 points
    Leading money winner: $18,358.00

1942/Los Angeles Open
    San Francisco Open
    Hale America Open
    North and South Open
    Asheville Open
    Rochester Open
    No Vardon Award made.
    Leading money winner: $13,143.00

1945/Nashville Open
    Portland Open
    Richmond Open
    Montgomery Open
    Orlando Open

1946/Phoenix Open
     Texas Open
     St. Petersburg Open
     Miami Four-Ball
     Colonial Invitational
     Western Open
     Goodall Round-Robin
     Inverness Four-Ball
     Winnipeg Open
     PGA Championship
     Golden State Championship
     Dallas Invitational
     North and South Open
     No Vardon Award made.
     Leading money winner: $42,556.00

1947/Los Angeles Open
     Phoenix Open
     Miami Four-Ball
     Colonial Invitational
     Chicago Open
     Inverness Four-Ball
     International Championship

1948/Los Angeles Open
     PGA Championship
     U. S. Open
     Motor City Open
     Western Open
     Inverness Four-Ball
     Reading Open
     Denver Open
     Reno Open
     Glendale Open
     Bing Crosby Pro-Amateur
     Winner: Vardon Trophy, 69.3 strokes per round
     Leading money winner: $32,112.00
     PGA Golfer of the Year

1949/Bing Crosby Invitational
     Long Beach Open

1950/Greenbrier Invitational
     U. S. Open
     PGA Golfer of the year

1951/Masters Tournament
     U. S. Open
     World's Championship
     PGA Golfer of the Year

1952/Colonial Invitational

1953/Masters Tournament
     Pan-American Open
     Colonial Invitational
     U. S. Open
     British Open
     PGA Golfer of the Year
     Professional Male Athlete of the Year

1956/Canada Cup
     International Trophy

1959/Colonial Invitational

SOURCES AND BIBLIOGRAPHY

Ben Hogan, *The Modern Fundamentals of Golf,* p. 1.
Conversation with newsmen, p. 13.
Conversation with the author, p. 23.
Sam Snead with Al Stump, *The Education of a Golfer,* p. 31.
Gene Sarazen with Herbert Warren Wind,
  Thirty Years of Championship Golf, p. 41.
Conversation with O. B. Keeler, p. 49.
Conversation with the author, p. 59.
Conversation with newsmen, p. 71.
"Views of Sport," New York *Herald-Tribune,*
January 12, 1950, p. 79.
Conversation with newsmen, p. 91.
Masters Tournament press booklet, p. 111.
Civic luncheon speech, Fort Worth, p. 127.
Conversation with the author, p. 137.
Telegram to Ben Hogan, p. 155
Conversation with the author, p. 163.
Conversation with the author, p. 171.

Jimmy Demaret, *My Partner, Ben Hogan.*
Tom Flaherty, *The U. S. Open, 1895–1965.*
Herb Graffis, *The PGA.*
Ben Hogan, *The Modern Fundamentals of Golf.*
———, *Power Golf.*
Mark H. McCormack, *The World of Professional Golf.*
Toney Penna, *My Wonderful World of Golf.*
Clifford Roberts, *The Story of the Augusta National Golf Club.*
Gene Sarazen with Herbert Warren Wind, *Thirty Years of Championship Golf.*
Sam Snead with Al Stump, *The Education of a Golfer.*
Herbert Warren Wind, *The Story of American Golf.*
———, ed., *The Complete Golfer.* An anthology.
———, ed., *The Realm of Sport.*

Golf Digest
Golfdom

Golfing
Golf Monthly (Edinburgh, Scotland)
Golf World
Life
The New Yorker
PGA Professional Golfer Magazine
Reader's Digest
Time
USGA Journal

Associated Press

Chicago *Daily News*
Chicago *Tribune*
Christian Science Monitor
Cleveland *Plain Dealer*
Denver *Post*
El Paso *Herald-Post*
El Paso *Times*
San Diego *Evening Tribune*
Fort Worth *Star-Telegram*
Greensboro, N.C.,*Daily News*
Los Angeles *Times*
New York *Daily News*
New York *Herald-Tribune*
New York *Post*
New York *Times*
New York *World-Telegram*
Phoenix *Republic*
San Antonio *Light*
San Diego *Union*
San Francisco *Chronicle*
Glasgow *Herald*
London *Daily Herald*
London *Daily Mail*
London *Daily Express*
London *Daily Telegraph*
London *News-Chronicle*
London *Times*

INDEX